I KNOW YOU CAN'T, BUT I CAN!!!

Jimmy Epting

Dedication

To my wife, Gretchen who has been my ministry partner for forty-five years. She is my soulmate and has been there for our family and me. Anything that I have accomplished should be accredited to the good Lord and her. She gave her whole life to family and most of her life to North Greenville University. She has entertained and fed hundreds, if not thousands, of friends, faculty, staff and students in our home without one complaint. Without a doubt she is a special lady who loves the Lord and serves Him well. I thank you for making the difference in my life.

Acknowledgements

I appreciate those who directly and indirectly made the difference in my ministry!

First, I want to thank my father, B.I. Epting, and my mother, Sara C. Epting, for providing a Christian home and being sure that church was where I belonged. He was my pastor and for many years she was my Sunday School teacher. They instilled in me the passion for lost souls and the importance of worshipping with other believers. Also, I am grateful for my sisters, Myra and Renee'. They always encouraged me to be the best in all of my endeavors. Dad, Mom, and Myra are celebrating in Heaven today!

Gretchens' parents, Paul and Daphne Moore, showed me how to care for and love others. They treated everyone better than themselves. Paul was not only my father-in-law, but one of my best friends. The Lord took him home in 1996 which left a huge void in my life and I miss him so much. Granny (Daphne) is 95 years old and is still making a tremendous difference for Jesus Christ. She continues to be an inspiration to me.

Gretchen is my very best friend and continues to be my encourager for sharing Jesus with others. It is an honor and privilege to dedicate this book to her.

My sons and their wives, Paul and Caroline and Bert and Hannah, have made me so proud and I am grateful for their commitment to Jesus Christ. They are involved in the local church and make a difference for Him.

Both Bert and Paul work for the Lord at Christ-centered universities and I could have never picked two better daughters-in-law. As a matter of fact God had to do it.

I thank God for nine healthy and beautiful grandchildren. I want them to love the Lord with all their heart, soul, strength and mind. Most important of all, I want them to know all the wonderful things God did through Nana and Pops at North Greenville University and the truth about everything!

Finally, I would be remiss if I did not thank those administrators, faculty, and staff who encouraged me to write this book. I sure do love and appreciate each of you.

Foreword

In 1990 my wife, Jeanette, and I were living in Conyers, GA during the years when I was on the staff of the Home Mission Board in Atlanta, now known as the North American Mission Board. We received a telephone call one day from Dr. Ray P. Rust, then the Executive Secretary – Treasurer of the South Carolina Baptist Convention. He said that he and Joy would be driving through Atlanta in a few days to see their loved ones in Louisiana and in Texas for a time of vacation. Dr. Rust said that they would like to visit with us on the way and asked if we could meet with them for lunch at a local restaurant because they would be passing near us off I-20.

We were delighted to receive their invitation and quickly agreed. I had come to know Dr. Rust very well because of the years I had served as the Regional Coordinator for planning and budgeting purposes of the Home Mission Board in relationship to the various Baptist state conventions up and down the eastern seaboard states plus Puerto Rico and the U.S. Virgin Islands. I had met with him and members of his staff at least twice a year in Columbia at the state convention building then located across from the governor's mansion. We were eager to see them.

During the time of our visit he said that he wanted to talk to me about moving back to my home state of South Carolina and becoming the assistant Executive Secretary-Treasurer of the state convention pending the upcoming retirement of Dr. E. C. Watson who held the position at that time. To say the least, I was surprised and honored. I thought so highly of Dr. Rust and certainly loved the South Carolina Baptist Convention. After a time of prayer and reflection, Jeanette and I concluded that we would accept the invitation if agreed upon by the General Board of Directors and the state convention. In due time the Board affirmed Dr. Rust's recommendation, and we soon moved to South Carolina.

One of my first intentions after I joined the staff was to visit the various institutions and agencies of the South Carolina Baptist Convention. I had grown up in Hartsville and had heard often of the various Baptist institutions and Baptist associates due to the fact that my home church, First Baptist, was a loyal and committed congregation to the total life and witness of South Carolina Baptists. I quickly made plans to visit the leaders of the four colleges, the two retirement homes, the children's home, the Baptist Courier, and Baptist hospital in addition to the various associational offices across the state as time allowed.

I remember that my first visit to one of the colleges was to Furman, and I was so impressed with the individuals and officials I met and certainly with the beautiful campus in every regard. Next I went to North Greenville Junior College at Tigerville and I was, to say the least, shocked and dismayed. The few buildings I saw on campus were in sad shape, and the grounds, shrubbery, and over-all landscaping were badly in need of attention. I remember thinking that surely South Carolina Baptists can do better than this! For some reason that day, I did not meet the new president, Dr. Jimmy Epting. He was probably away on college business. I just went to the campus unannounced and simply drove around and then walked around. I left somewhat saddened and discouraged by the appearance of one of our schools.

In about a year or so, Dr. Rust announced his intention to retire. Needless to say, I was surprised. I had not been there that long and he was retiring? I could not talk him out of it even though I surely did try. In time the General Board, as it was known then, voted to recommend me to succeed Dr. Rust if approved by the South Carolina Baptist Convention in annual session. He and I had never discussed such a possibility. I was honored to become in 1992 by a unanimous vote of the state convention the next Executive Director-Treasurer of my beloved South Carolina Baptist Convention.

Soon after, the administrative committee of the Board met at the convention building for a regularly scheduled meeting. On the agenda was an item to discuss the future of North Greenville Junior College in relationship to the state convention. Dr. Epting was asked to meet with the committee. I had never had a conversation with him before, and I was surprised at his appearance. He looked tired, worn out, and discouraged. I listened with the committee to Dr.

Epting's presentation about the status of North Greenville and his plea for the Board to continue sponsoring the school and give him more time to turn the situation around if at all possible. As I recall, the men and women listened to him politely and then asked him to leave the room. It appeared to me that everyone's mind was made up to vote to cease Cooperative Program funding. If so, such a move would obviously close the school.

I recall sitting there around the large conference table as a motion and a second was made, and the chairman asked if anyone had anything else to say before the vote. I said that I did and asked the committee to hear me out. I simply indicated that I did not really know Dr. Epting and that I knew the sad condition of the college because I had been there. I went on to say how impressed I was by his vision for the school which he presented to us that day. I asked the committee to delay the vote and give Dr. Epting along with my support the opportunity to see if there might be any chance that the school could be saved and put in a positive position for the future. I also said that I promised that in a year if North Greenville continued to be in a declining situation, I would return to the committee and recommend that North Greenville be closed.

As I recollect, Rev. David Hull, at that time the pastor of First Baptist Church of Laurens and a member of the Board, responded by saying to the committee, "I agree that North Greenville is on its last leg, but Dr. Epting is still new at it and Dr. Driggers is new in his position, so I make a substitute motion that we table the vote for one year and give them a chance to work at it and see if the college might survive and begin to show needed improvements in many ways." After a moment of quiet reflection and some discussion, the motion passed unanimously, and the rest is history. The motion to discontinue North Greenville never came up again in future meetings due to the marvelous progress of the school under the leadership of Dr. Epting.

I am convinced that God intervened, and North Greenville College soon began to emerge out of the pit of despair and hopelessness. I used to watch and pray that not only would North Greenville survive and thrive but that Dr. Epting would, also, because he worked so hard for the school and for South Carolina Baptists. I paid attention, as well, as he and Gretchen drove over the state in an older, dilapidated looking Mercury sedan to promote the school, raise funds, and seek students. In time, North Greenville Junior College became North Greenville University as a four year school, and donor after donor stepped up to provide urgently needed funds, often by the millions. I observed how the campus grew to become a thriving and outstanding South Carolina Baptist institution of higher learning along with our other two fine schools: Charleston Southern University, led by Dr. Jairy Hunter who retired in 2018 and Anderson University, led for a few years by Dr. Lee Royce who went on to become president of Mississippi Baptist College. He was followed by the current president, Dr. Evans Whitaker. Those former presidents – Dr. Hunter, Dr. Royce and Dr. Epting – provided marvelous leadership for their schools, and Dr. Whitaker continues to do so at Anderson. I so appreciate and respect those presidents. It was an honor for me to relate to them and keep Cooperative Program funds from South Carolina Baptist churches flowing to the schools for stability and advancement to the glory of God. May I say at this point that no one could be more affirming than I was and continue to be about all of our South Carolina Baptist institutions which include Connie Maxwell Children's Home, Martha Franks and Bethea Retirement Homes, in addition to the Baptist Foundation of the South Carolina Baptist Convention, and the Baptist Courier. All of them should make every South Carolina Baptist grateful and proud.

One of my most memorable recollections from my visit to campus during Dr. Epting's tenure was the interactions of the students with him, both male and female. From time to time, I would visit North Greenville as I did with all our institutions, perhaps to make a casual appearance, but at other times for some item of importance. When I would visit Dr. Epting, I noticed that we could hardly walk across campus or through the hallway of the administration building or at the cafeteria without students coming up to him and saying something like, "Mr. President, I need a hug today!" I thoroughly enjoyed watching those interchanges but, I must admit, at times I became a little impatient because I needed to complete my visit with him so I could go on to my next engagement somewhere in the state. All that interaction between the president and the students would delay me! However, those times between the students and their president were most inspiring to me. It was affirming to say the least and encouraging to observe.

The book Dr. Epting has written is a very personal and heartfelt accounting of his service at North Greenville. It is thoughtfully written and certainly gives a worthy description of the progress attained during his years as president. He makes clear his love for the school and his deep regret for the way his tenure came to a close. May I say that what he has written appears to me to be in two distinct parts. The first part is to page 126 which is without a doubt marvelous reading, full of inspiring stories and wonderful, appropriate illustrations.

Then all of a sudden the account changes, and the remarkable progress and the affirmation of the previous pages become overshadowed and questionable. What happened? The story becomes sad and raises serious questions about the close of Dr. Epting's tenure at North Greenville University. For a fact, the majority of his years of service and leadership were outstanding and honored the Lord and South Carolina Baptists. From my standpoint, President James B. Epting did a remarkable work at the school, but it ended far too soon. I regret it deeply. I so wish it could have been different. For me, personally, I choose to remember the good over the bad, and I pray that the best of God's blessings will be with the Epting family and certainly with North Greenville University during the years ahead.

May I also request of the readers of the book that those of us who know and love Gretchen and Jimmy Epting covenant together and pray for them that any estrangement from their daughter and her family may soon be healed to the glory of God.

Dr. B. Carlisle Driggers
Executive Director-Treasurer Emeritus
South Carolina Baptist Convention

Endorsements

The instant I met Jimmy Epting I knew. There was no doubt God's hand was on him. Furthermore, there was no doubt he was a man on a mission for the Lord Jesus Christ. Jimmy's call in life has always been to serve the Lord. His mission is "just one more!" "Christ is our only hope."

This combination expresses itself through his incredible leadership and immense administrative giftedness. It is no wonder that North Greenville University rose up from the ashes to become a leading force in kingdom work. Yes, from ball games, to buildings, to academic excellence for sure, NGU is where "Christ Makes the Difference."

Jimmy Epting's passion for Christ and his fellow man is undiminished. His seat and his circumstances may have changed, but not Jimmy Epting. This book recounts his amazing story. It is well worth reading

Dr. Don Wilton
Senior Pastor of First Baptist Church, Spartanburg, SC
Founder and President of The Encouraging Word

While working as the personal assistant to Dr. Charles Stanley, I was afforded the opportunity to, not only travel across the globe, but to meet many great leaders. One of those leaders was Jimmy Epting. Jimmy is one of those people who never meets a stranger and I count his friendship as one of my greatest blessings.

Over the years, my wife and I have enjoyed countless hours in the company of Jimmy and Gretchen. During those times, they humbly shared what God had done and what God was doing at NGU. He always says, "Just one more for Christ." That was, and still is, his number one mission and he is faithful to put those words into action. I have seen firsthand, Jimmy bring those words to life through his commitment to the Lord, NGU, and the students, always giving God the glory for providing for every need time and time again. God's provision was made apparent. This book reflects Jimmy's passion for God and his deep love for NGU.

Bob Schipper,
Retired Executive Assistant to Dr. Charles Stanley

When you hear of North Greenville University, you can't help but be reminded of the great miracles God has done through His faithful servant Jimmy Epting. God took a man in love with Him and in love with people to revive a dying college to become one of the foremost equipping stations for men and women to spread the gospel of the Lord Jesus Christ to the "uttermost parts of the world". *I Know You Can't, But I Can!!!* is the wonderful story of these miracles.

Rev. Joe F. Hayes, Jr., Retired,
Pastor and Executive Director at North Greenville University

Rarely would I use the word "miraculous" to describe changes that occurred in an educational institution. But I can't think of a more accurate word to describe the turnaround that took place at North Greenville University under the leadership of Dr. James "Jimmy" B. Epting. In *I Know You Can't, But I Can!!!* Jimmy pulls back the curtain and shares behind-the-scene stories and details that reveal why many South Carolina Baptists consider North Greenville's transformation a miracle.

As the title indicates, Jimmy is the first to give glory to God for all that happened to transform that struggling little college with one-foot-in-the-grave into a respected, thriving university where "Christ Makes the Difference." While all the glory rightly belongs to God, the

Lord obviously chose to use Jimmy Epting as His human instrument to lead North Greenville through the battles and blessings of change and growth.

As you read Jimmy's story, you will be surprised and saddened to learn of some of the battles that he and others had to fight to make a Baptist college a place where "Christ Makes the Difference." But you will also be overwhelmed and overjoyed when you read of the unexpected but timely blessings that came in ways that could only be explained as God's gracious and miraculous intervention.

You do not have to be associated with an educational institution to be blessed by my friend Jimmy Epting's new book, *I Know You Can't, But I Can!!!* As much as anything, it's a story about God's providential and amazing work in and through a man who knew that, while there were limits on what he could do, there were no limits on what the Lord Jesus Christ could do through him.

Dr. Fred G. Stone
Pastor, First Baptist Church, Pickens, SC

Dr. James B. (Jimmy) Epting is one of the most effective leaders I have met in three decades of ministry. All who know him would agree that time spent with Epting leaves you motivated and inspired to become more like Jesus Christ. In addition to his achievements in academia, Jimmy Epting is a truly amazing ambassador for the Gospel.

But even the most faithful servants sometime suffer through severe personal trials. Epting's career could fill textbooks on academic administration and leadership in general. And yet, after miraculously saving a university from certain demise, growing the school into a nationally-known contender among Christian colleges, and investing their lives on behalf of others ... the Eptings weathered a season of unimaginable betrayal and heartbreak.

But, *I Know You Can't, But I Can!!!* (which is Dr. Epting's story) is ultimately one of hope and victory. That is because the Epting's journey of life and ministry remains solidly focused on the goodness of God. *I Know You Can't, But I Can!!!* is a riveting book that will inspire, inform, and convict all who read it. And like Dr. Epting himself, the book will turn your attention toward Jesus. I enthusiastically commend to you this book and its author; Each has impacted my life significantly.

Rev. Alex McFarland,
Evangelist, Author, Broadcaster

I have known Dr. Epting for over 24 years and he has been instrumental in not only my life and my family's life, but literally thousands who serve Jesus around the world. God has and still uses his life to challenge many as well as be an incredible example of integrity and God's ability to do the impossible as this book projects. God used him incredibly to carve a great University out of a seemingly impossible task. You will be challenged to see what God can do through your life as you read this book.

Rev. Murrill Boitnott,
Retired, Founder of Macedonian Call,
Staff Evangelist at North Greenville University, Pastor

The story of North Greenville University is one that should resonate with every alumni and South Carolina Baptist. What God has done on that campus in the hearts and lives of so many students is truly a miracle. I count it a blessing to be a part of the North Greenville family and I am grateful for the impact that North Greenville and Dr. Jimmy Epting continues to have on my life!

Rev. Benjamin Smoak,
Pastor, Mountain Springs Baptist Church

Contents

Chapter 1
OBEDIENT TO THE CALL

On December 18, 1990, the Chairman of the Board of Trustees at North Greenville College, Dr. Russell Ashmore, called me and wanted to talk. In our meeting, he mentioned that the problems at the college were very serious. I made a few suggestions and discussed my happiness in my present job, but never mentioned returning to North Greenville. Then, one month later, I received another call about getting together, and we met on January 22, 1991. He wanted to know if I would be interested in coming back as president, because the board was going to make a change at the top. I again indicated my satisfaction with my current position and that someone else would do a better job. We discussed the college's problems thoroughly, and I made it abundantly clear what needed to be done in order to save it. Some of my suggestions and recommendations were:

- Hire a new president.
- Eliminate all the vice presidents and many other positions.
- Go see people, and ask for money.
- Make a stronger commitment to Jesus Christ – develop a distinctiveness and uniqueness through a commitment to quality education in a biblically sound, Christ-centered environment. The college would need to be a place where "Christ makes the difference." Jesus Christ would be the head and center of all our thinking. We should care as much for the spiritual well-being of our students as their academic achievements. Only Christians should be hired to work at North Greenville. We should have prayer and devotion before

1

all classes, games, practices, programs, and activities. There will be no planned or required activities on Sunday. We will have two chapels each week with emphasis on evangelism and missions. There should be a strong integration of faith and learning and a Christian worldview. The commitment to Global Missions should be tremendously improved. The college should work hard in partnership with South Carolina Baptists, be in more churches, and see more pastors.

- Declare financial exigency and let everyone know the college's bad state of finances. The college must cut back on all spending.
- Become a four-year institution by starting with church-related vocation programs.
- The board and administration should take charge of the institution and strongly encourage the faculty to teach and love the students.
- The development of the total student – spiritually, socially, physically, and mentally – is imperative.
- It is a privilege to have the opportunity to attend North Greenville College. If a student violates the major rules, he or she must return home – no exceptions.
- Strengthen the involvement of the faculty outside the classroom.
- All vocations will need to be seen as Christian vocations.
- Place more emphasis on academics and raise admission standards.
- Raise athletic standards and expectations.

North Greenville College would need a new beginning with a thorough cleansing. It was time to cut back to the roots and be proud of its Baptist heritage – build a new institution for God!

On February 1, 1991, the Executive Committee of the Board of Trustees met to discuss the college's future, which might include me as the next president. After the meeting, I was informed that the current president would be asked to resign the next week at the full board meeting. Then, they planned to ask me to pray and consider becoming the new president. Since God always knows best, He sent snow to Tigerville, South Carolina, where North Greenville College is located, and the meeting was cancelled for another week. Before the rescheduled meeting, the current president resigned, and the possibility of me becoming the next president spread like wildfire. Many concerns were raised about me and the possibility of not having a search committee. Therefore, these concerns led to a committee made up of administration, faculty, board, alumni, students, and staff members. When told about the change in plans concerning the opportunity, I wished them well and made it clear that I would NOT be applying for the job. I felt that God was closing the door for me, and I had learned a long time ago that one should not try to knock down or go through any doors He closed.

Dr. Ashmore asked me numerous times for a résumé, but I refused and told him again that I was not applying for the position. I found out later that one of my friends sent them an old résumé of mine. Then, the Search Committee Chairman, Dr. Bruce Russell, informed me that I was one of three finalists, and he wanted me to interview with the committee. In the meantime, my family and I were being ostracized by the faculty and some of the staff. Some of the statements we heard were:

- I was campaigning for the job
- I cared only about athletics and not academics
- I would make North Greenville a bible college
- I embezzled money when I worked at the college before
- I mistreated the staff, faculty, and students

These were just a few of the most widely shared comments. A few of the faculty called a faculty-wide meeting to criticize me and to approve a resolution against considering me for the presidency. It was reported that only one dear faculty member, Mrs. Doris Tingle, had the courage to defend me in this meeting. They called all the trustees with these and many more accusations, and demanded that I not even be considered for the job. It became a very unprofessional mess, and if nothing else, it left me with no choice but to interview for the purpose of clearing my name, as well as defending my family.

Due to all the above, the search committee would not meet with me on campus, and set up a meeting at Taylors First Baptist Church, which was 20 minutes away from North Greenville College. The administrator on the committee had already indicated displeasure with my consideration, and refused to attend the interview. During the interview, only two out of the group were belligerent to me, and their behavior caused the others to appreciate me being there even more. I shared **The New Beginning Plan** and was emphatic about what would need to be done. The committee members shared my vision and plans with others and it turned the naysayers even more against me – so they turned the heat up in opposition.

On April 10, 1991, Dr. Ashmore and Dr. Russell met with me to investigate the accusations and seek the truth. After a thorough examination of my past, they offered me the position subject to approval of the full board of trustees. Although I did not think the good Lord wanted me to be the next president after all that had happened, I remained on my knees and in the scriptures, seeking to be obedient to the call to serve either here or in my present job, or elsewhere.

Most importantly, I needed to keep everything in proper perspective. Many times, especially in leadership roles, it becomes more about the person and less about God. I am reminded of the letter from a young lady who had been at college for several months without making any contact with her parents. This is hard for me to imagine, since all my children, when in college, called on a regular basis for the sole purpose of asking for money, and then (second), mentioning that they loved me. Finally, she wrote this letter:

Dear Mom and Dad:

I'm sorry to be so long in writing, but all my writing paper was lost the night the dormitory was burned down by the demonstrators. I'm out of the hospital now and the doctor says my eyesight should be back to normal sooner or later. The wonderful boy, Bill, who rescued me from the fire, kindly offered to share his little apartment with me until the dorm is rebuilt. He comes from a good family, so you won't be surprised when I tell you we are going to get married. In fact, you always wanted a grandchild, so you will be glad to know you will be grandparents in a few months.

Love, Sue

Then she added this P.S.:

*Please disregard the above practice in English Composition. There was no fire. I haven't been in the hospital. I'm not going to have a child. I'm not getting married, and I don't even have a steady boyfriend. **But**, I did get a D in French and an F in Chemistry. I just wanted you to know how much worse it could have been!"*

Obviously, the girl wanted her parents to have a proper perspective; but, you really don't have to exaggerate or concoct a wild story to get a proper perspective on the challenge of leading a dying institution. It did help my perspective when I received a copy of a resolution sent to the board of trustees from almost all of the staff, supporting me for the presidency.

My wife, Gretchen, was so supportive during this very difficult time, as we tried to make this life-changing decision. She helped us keep things in proper prospective by helping me realize that Jesus Christ is in control. Her Christian walk was and still is an inspiration to the family and me. She was willing to serve with me if He called us!

Even with constant prayer, quiet time with God, and searching the scriptures, I could not discern what God wanted me to do. So, one day I called my dad and told him they wanted me to be the next president of North Greenville College. He immediately dropped the phone and in disbelief, picked it up and said, "They want you?" I told him that his response was not funny and I needed his advice. First, he referred to my searching God's Word and praying.

Then, he said, "Son, if you will remember, after serving my country in the war, God saved me and called me to preach. No other school would take my family or me except North Greenville College. We graduated from there, Furman University, and the Southern Baptist Theological Seminary. I have been a South Carolina Baptist pastor most of my life, and I am still *obedient to the call to serve.* If it had not been for North Greenville Junior College, I would have never had the opportunity. I know that little school on the hill in a dark corner of South Carolina is having a difficult time, but I cannot believe the good Lord is through with it. **It has done too much good for too many good people.** You will just have to continue praying and seeking God's will in this matter." It was amazing that I was called to the school where my family started their Christ-centered journey!

Since God does not talk to me audibly like He did to so many in the Bible, it encouraged me to seek His face even more. For you see, I like the way God does it. If He had a phone where we could call Him each and every day, it would go something like this: we would pick up the phone and say, "Hey Lord, How are you? Oh, it's so good to talk to you today, and I just want to tell you about some of my concerns… I need some answers to my questions," and then, "thank you, Lord for talking to me." If it were that easy, I would probably just hang the phone up and not talk to Him again. So the way God has it set up, I have to spend time during the day on my knees and in His Word, and perhaps, spend a lot more time with Him than merely picking up the phone one day a week.

During this time of decision, I was working at Furman University as Executive Director for the Paladin Club and helping with their campaign. One of my mentors was the president, Dr. John Johns. We had a special relationship in spite of our many differences. For example, I was more conservative and he was more moderate. I will never forget the day he came to my office and told me to clear my calendar because he was going to take me to lunch. Over the three-hour lunch, we discussed the pros and cons concerning the opportunity at North Greenville College.

Finally, he looked at me and said, "Jimmy, you should take the job. If the school closes, then it is not your fault and everyone will say that you made a gallant effort. If it survives, then you will be the hero. As far as I am concerned, you cannot lose. But, most importantly, if the worst happens, I will give you your job back at Furman." To say the least, his confidence in me was reassuring and made a difference as I was trying to make the decision.

One morning I did something I knew no one else would do and many would recommend as not the best way to make a decision. I closed my eyes, opened my Bible, and pointed my finger where I had opened it. My finger was sitting on Luke 10:27, and it read, "So he answered and said, 'You shall love the Lord your God with all your heart, with all your soul, with all your strength, and with all your mind,' and 'your neighbor as yourself.'" Now I had seen this verse many times over the years, but circumstances in your life will cause God's Word to come across differently and help you keep things in proper perspective. I could not understand why God was allowing me to suffer such persecution from others concerning this opportunity, which was causing me to not see His will for my life. Immediately, I realized that, if I was going to be the next president of North Greenville College, my commitment and North Greenville's commitment to Jesus Christ would have to be stronger than ever before. It meant giving our all at all costs. My dad gave me the best definition for commitment; I am sure he heard it from someone else, but it goes like this: "When you think of commitment, you should remember the **hen** and the **hog**. We certainly want the hen to lay eggs and we are proud of her efforts; it comes so naturally with dedication. Then, she carries on with life. But, when the hog gives a ham, now that's commitment."

Now please do not misunderstand; Jesus Christ came into my heart at a very early age and I believe the Bible teaches the eternal security of all believers. Up to this time, I had tried to live for Him in every way and was very active serving in my church. I was so proud of all the good things I was doing – teaching Sunday School, Discipleship Training, and Royal Ambassadors. I was a deacon and sang in the choir. I almost broke my arm trying to pat myself on the back for my good service! Also, North Greenville College was a good Baptist school and played the religious card well. But God was making it clear that He wanted me to serve as president only if both of us (the school and myself) were willing to **cut it up a notch** for Him. He was not asking, He was telling. When I was growing up, we did not have time to ask, "Please turn out the light." We got to the issue quickly by saying, "Cut it off," as well as "do it now." God was saying that the plan is solid and we must be committed to being passionate about it.

Loving our God requires our all – heart, soul, strength, and mind – that is everything. Then God says to love your neighbor as yourself. What right do we have to keep Him to ourselves? If there was to be a future for North Greenville College, and if I were to be the leader, we had to have a real **passion for lost souls**! Three things had to happen: the student, if not saved when arriving as a student, needed to have the opportunity to get saved; or if already saved, become stronger in their walk; and they must do well academically to graduate. These could all happen at the same time without hurting the quality of academic programs. As a matter of fact, they would enhance it.

Second, we had to have a strong passion for God's love as the key to North Greenville being a family. Also, it became evident to me that the best way to express His love to the family was the "**HUG**." Thus, the "Jimmy Hug" became a part of the everyday life of the family at North Greenville.

As one can see, after reading Luke 10:27, I felt that God was calling me to serve Him as North Greenville College's president, and to help this institution be stronger at representing Him. On April 17, 1991, my wife and I were presented to the Board of Trustees. There were two votes against us on the first vote, and then they asked for another vote so the decision would be unanimous. The board had elected me as the 7th president of North Greenville College. Also, they approved the adoption of *The New Beginning Plan* and agreed to accept all decisions of the president during this time of transition and survival. Then, we were presented to the North Greenville College family. It was obvious who was in favor of the decision by the Search Committee and the Board of Trustees, and who was against it. I am possibly the only university president who received a vote of no-confidence from the faculty before taking the job.

It became apparent that, if I were to be an effective leader, it had to be about Him and not me. I had to have humility. I needed to surround myself with good people. I had to be relentless about the plan and build momentum with it. I had to have commitment and passion. I should confront the brutal facts and be willing to take risks. I had to have vision and be consistent with it. Most importantly, I needed to be obedient to the *call to serve.*

On April 22, 1991, we had our first Executive Committee of the Board meeting and a press conference to introduce me as president of North Greenville College. At the board meeting when they voted on me, and at the Executive Committee meeting, we spent a major part of the meetings on our knees seeking the face and mind of God. Obviously, to those who are Christians, **prayer is the number one key to effective leadership and good decisions.**

Sculpture on campus of the Leader on His Knees
(Jesus said, "I know you can't, but I can!!!")

By the end of my first day on May 1, 1991, I was on my knees with tears flowing down my face. I was telling God that I could not do this job. It was the hardest day of my life, before or since. I felt His Spirit saying, *"I know you can't, but I can!!!"* My prayer was for **God to do something so big and in such a way that no man could take credit for it. He made it very clear that if I would seek His face and mind, all things would be possible through Him.**

Chapter 2
SURVIVING / STABILIZING
/ THRIVING

On the first day as president, I had to declare financial exigency (emergency). I would have to eliminate over fifteen positions, including all the vice presidents. Each person was informed of their termination and encouraged to spend the rest of the month looking for another job, because their salary would end on May 31. During the first year, many positions were eliminated in our effort to reduce the budget by $1 million.

At this time, I found that familiarity was the first key to survival for the institution. The college did not have time for someone to have a one-year honeymoon before making difficult decisions. I had previously served as Dean of Students, Instructor, Athletic Director, Vice President for Student Development, and Vice President for Institutional Advancement for twelve years at North Greenville College, before leaving to work in development at another private Baptist university, Furman, for almost one year. **I had a clear understanding of the problems and could better facilitate the necessary changes.**

After sharing with the Board of Trustees the vision of a new purpose, which was **"A New Beginning"** plan that involved difficult decisions to cut the institution back to the roots, they accepted it and unanimously agreed to support all my decisions as president.

In order to save the college, it was imperative that the board approve the plan, establish policy, and allow the president to operate without restraints. Therefore, it was now the opportune time to get on our knees and turn everything over to God. We started our journey together in prayer, asking God to direct our every step with His will being done – not ours. We also asked for wisdom, understanding, knowledge, and discernment for me as president. From that point, no decisions were made without seeking God's guidance. **If God brings you to it, He will bring you through it.**

As my first day was coming to an end, and I was feeling sorry for myself, I quickly realized that North Greenville College just might close. The South Carolina Baptist leaders had decided that it was time to close the smallest of their four institutions of higher learning. North Greenville College had only 329 students, was $3 million in debt, and could not make payroll nor pay the bills. The buildings on campus were also in dire need of renovation. While understanding this reality, it was abundantly clear that **God had called me to be the servant leader, and to help Him make the difference. It would be a privilege to serve, realizing that He could have chosen anyone, but He chose me. One must remember that God never calls one to do anything he or she can do on their own. If He did, they would not need God. It was important that I followed God's will rather than seek a position. I knew that God does not necessarily call the equipped, but equips the called!**

The second morning on the job, a friend came to my office with a placard that said, "I can do all things through Christ who strengthens me." – Philippians 4:13. Without a doubt, this act confirmed my interpretation of what the Spirit was saying to me: **"I know you can't, but I can!!!"** Over the next couple of weeks, I met with every person employed by the college to verify verbally that Jesus Christ was in their heart and to ascertain their commitment to the mission of the school. A number of them had to be dismissed from the college because their answers were not affirming. The ones who stayed had to also feel called to **"wash other people's feet"** and to be **"prayer warriors."**

We expected the occurrence of prayer and devotion at the beginning of every class, meeting, and practice. We required the integration of faith and learning in all course work, activities, and programs, meaning that Jesus Christ had to be central to all aspects of the college. Many colleges, public and private, have pockets of

Christianity, such as a collegiate ministry or Fellowship of Christian Athletes (FCA) club, but Christ-centeredness at these colleges is usually a window dressing when it comes to true integration. Therefore, all the above would form our foundation and shape our purpose.

During the first few months on the job, I did not hang any of my pictures on the wall, because I was not sure how long the college would survive. In one of my quiet times with God, I simply mentioned that if He would provide a center-piece for my wall, I could hang the other pictures. It would also be an encouragement that all is well concerning our future. For obvious reasons, I was trying to speak every Sunday in a church. On one particular Sunday in a local church, the pastor invited me to have lunch with the youth after the service, so I could recruit them. In lieu of an honorarium, they gave me a large framed picture, which was the exact size needed for a center-piece. More importantly, it was a picture of Jesus earnestly counseling a man at his desk and the inscription at the bottom stated, "Thou shalt guide me with thy counsel, and afterward receive me to glory." – Psalm 73:24 (KJV).

THOU SHALT GUIDE ME WITH THY COUNSEL,
AND AFTERWARD RECEIVE ME TO GLORY
Psalm 73:24

This act of kindness by the youth not only confirmed our survival, but God spoke to me through this picture and verse. I realized that **I must seek His counsel at all times, and attempt something so impossible, that unless God is in it, it's doomed for failure.** We are often tempted to just settle for what is - for the status quo.

In order for North Greenville College to first survive, then stabilize, and eventually thrive, I needed to have a genuine passion for the new mission with a clear vision of that mission. The mission was articulated thus: "to offer quality education in a biblically sound, Christ-centered environment." We wanted to be a place where Jesus Christ makes the difference. To survive, we needed to be unique when compared to all other colleges and universities. As a conservative, evangelical, Christ-centered liberal arts college, we had to have an unapologetic **passion for lost souls.** Each and every student attending our college was encouraged to accept Jesus Christ into his or her heart and/or become stronger in their walk with Him, as well as graduate. Only then will we fulfill our mission.

It is important to know that the Board of Trustees had to accept, adopt, and enforce the following plan, **"A New Beginning,"** before I would agree to serve (the only changes to the plan over the years were pertaining to the four-year university status):

> Purpose: Affiliated with and committed to the South Carolina Baptist Convention, North Greenville College is a small two-year, co-educational liberal arts college which provides opportunities for higher education in a Christian atmosphere. The college strives to prepare students to become better, contributing members of society by educating the whole person through an integration of academic discipline, a Christian lifestyle, and an enriched cultural experience as well as offer students the best opportunities for spiritual growth, academic training, and Christian service.
>
> Christ must be the center of the campus for the purpose of Christian education/Christian character-building.

The College endeavors to serve these purposes by:

1. Offering the basic liberal arts curriculum, which not only builds the foundation for career-oriented programs, but also prepares students to transfer to institutions awarding the baccalaureate degree;

2. Offering limited career programs to students who wish to terminate their formal education with the associate degree;

3. Maintaining the college's heritage of providing quality education for under-prepared students, while continuing to strengthen opportunities to meet the needs of advanced and gifted students;

4. Presenting distinctive, innovative programs, which attract and meet the needs of non-traditional students;

5. Achieving high academic standards through the employment of qualified professionals and through furnishing appropriate educational support services;

6. Providing an environment in which students can realize their fullest potential as complete persons, developing intellectually, physically, socially, morally, and spiritually; and

7. Affording a special sense of community through the development of close personal relationships and the nurturing efforts of a caring, Christian, and dedicated faculty, staff, and administration.

As a Christian college, North Greenville College must keep the emphasis upon the work and person of Christ as the Son of God, Savior, and Lord. The college is Christian when Jesus Christ is head and center of all its thinking. The main purpose is to bring all of its students to a saving knowledge of Jesus Christ and a personal experience with Him. An education at North Greenville College is regarded as preparation for effective Christian service and witness. The Bible as the inspired and infallible word of God is the foundation of the curriculum and the basis of the philosophy of education and of life.

We care about the spiritual well-being of our students as well as their academic achievements.

Further, let it be understood that attendance at North Greenville College is a <u>privilege</u> and not a right, which may be forfeited by any student who does not conform to the standards and regulations of the institution. The College may request the withdrawal of any student at any time, who, in the opinion of the College, does not fit into the spirit of the institution, regardless of whether or not he/she conforms to specific rules and regulations of the College.

As we hired new faculty, staff, and administrators, considerations were given to Christ-centered individuals involved in their church who had high moral and personal ethics. We realized that the involvement of all employees with students outside of the classroom was vital to our success. In addition, we gradually strengthened the admission standards for acceptance.

During the first two years, I had to be willing to take risks and work hard at building a team. As I trusted God, I took those risks, and I sought humbly to serve others. I learned to surround myself with strong team members who assisted me in carrying out the vision. The individuals who God called to serve on His team were all more capable and qualified than I. Therefore, it was easy to share the responsibility and authority with them. Also, I came to understand that **trusting God means looking beyond what we can see to what God sees.**

This team was called the Executive Council and represented all areas of the college. The changes I made were based on three concepts: 1) some members of the team be North Greenville College graduates, 2) the ministries, on and off campus, be well represented, and 3) money be saved with each personnel decision. From these concepts, I made these crucial decisions:

- I fired the Vice President of Business Affairs and replaced him with the Business Manager. She became the Executive Director for Business Affairs and was paid approximately half the salary of the Vice President. In addition, I did not fill the position of Business Manager. This one decision saved the college approximately $60,000.

- I followed the above procedure with many of the Vice President positions – promoting assistants at a lower salary and not hiring for their positions.

- In most cases, these individuals were graduates and committed to our success.

- A campus minister was hired to be a member of the Executive Council, with responsibility of keeping Jesus Christ firmly on our campus, and an Executive Director for Denominational Relations became a member of our team with the responsibility of spreading the message of Jesus Christ through the many ministry programs off our campus.

- The Executive Council included the following: President, Executive Director for Academics and Student Life, Executive Director for Admissions and Financial Planning, Campus Minister, Executive Director for Denominational Relations, Executive Director for Development, and Executive Director for Business Affairs.

In addition, my first priority was to equip them, which involved praying for them, instructing, educating, and encouraging them to serve. As I empowered this team, I also made sure to hold each team member accountable for his or her actions. Finally, concerning the team concept, it was vital to create a sense of togetherness, which kept me from feeling lonely at the top.

Now, the team could work together to market the mission to the student. We wanted to be *user friendly* with a strong emphasis on the *student as the customer*. Obviously, we identified our number one market as the South Carolina Baptist student. If we could attract these students and retain them, then our success rate would be magnified. Also, since our focus was changing lives for Jesus Christ, we knew in essence that we could grow the college with "lost people." This genuine passion for lost souls would multiply our numbers into serious increases each year. Our approach was for every major and program, as well as everything we did, to proceed with the purpose of focusing on Jesus Christ. If it did not fulfill this purpose, we would discontinue it. Each student would be accepted on the basis of class rank, college prep course grades, and S.A.T. or A.C.T scores. With these requirements for acceptance, we started having better students. In addition, the student was required to sign an agreement that stated he or she understood all rules and regulations. Each student realized that North Greenville College is a Christ-centered college and it was a privilege to attend. Also, if he/she is guilty of violating one of the major rules, he or she will withdraw from the institution. We became serious about providing an environment that was conducive to good learning.

In light of our desire to be excellent academically and spiritually, we mandated chapel twice a week, required attendance at cultural events, and a campus wide curfew and dress code were implemented. Campus life improved. To link with the state Southern Baptist churches, it was decided, at the time, that all athletic teams, music groups, and any other representative groups at North Greenville College had to be composed of 60% South Carolina Baptist students. Also, to encourage church attendance and Christian principles, we discontinued any athletic practices or games on Sunday. All these changes and improvements made North Greenville College more unique, and different from all other colleges and universities, which made us attractive to the conservative, Christ-centered market. This spiritual tide caused a ripple effect that expanded our market to other states and countries. On a daily basis, we also did not try to be all things to all people. As a result, when students arrived on campus, they found a college that was the same as advertised – no surprises. I learned that the best advertisement is a satisfied customer.

In 1992, after a turbulent first year, we made our move to become a four-year college and began with two majors – Christian Studies and Church Music. We knew that we had to move slowly in order for the transition to be smooth.

After we made the decision to become a four-year college, we had to obtain approval from the Southern Association of Colleges and Schools (SACS) in order to make this substantive change. The annual meeting was being held in Norfolk, Virginia, at a downtown hotel. Two of my administrators and I drove up and stayed in a Red Carpet Inn, because we did not have the necessary funds to take a plane or stay in an expensive hotel. The next day, we arrived at the hotel early and tried to appear as though we had spent the night there by loitering around the lobby before our meeting with the SACS committee. Later that morning, we entered the room to plead our case for approval to begin the two four-year majors before approximately 50 people, set up in a congressional-style hearing. They asked many questions, and I certainly wanted to avoid any questions about finances. But, to my dismay, one of the committee members mentioned that he noticed a tremendous deficit in 1991. He asked how our finances would be for 1992. At that very moment, I firmly believed that God impressed upon me to say, "Well sir, if we are just one dollar in the black, I will thank the Lord!" The room became frighteningly quiet until I heard one snicker on the left, one on the right, and then everyone started laughing. I just knew that I had blown it as the laughter died down, until the same committee member said, "Young man, don't let our laughter bother you; all of us in this room know exactly how you feel." Immediately after leaving the room, I knew that God had performed another miracle – the committee approved our change.

Also, it was important to draw from a position of strength. In the college's past, the greatest success was the training of full-time Christian workers. Since the founding in 1892, North Greenville College has had many ministers and missionaries graduate and serve well. **It certainly was obvious, in order for me to be an effective leader, that I needed to learn from the past successes and failures, which would allow me to see clearer the direction to follow in the future. Also, I realized that faith and courage, a compelling vision, and genuine love for this institution were indispensable ingredients.** The stronger focus on Jesus Christ and the smooth transition to a four-year liberal arts college were major factors in leading North Greenville College from surviving through stabilizing to thriving. And He said, **"I know you can't, but I can!!!"**

Concerning academics, it also needs to be mentioned that in our four-year programs, all full-time professors had to have their doctorate degree. This policy gave instant credibility to the first part of our mission statement – a commitment to quality education.

After clearly positioning the college in the right market, and developing an aggressive admissions team who were trained to promote the intangibles, the enrollment increased for the August 1991 semester and increased every year of my presidency.

North Greenville University Enrollment 1990 to 2014

	Fall	Spring
1990-1991	392	329
1991-1992	386	359
1992-1993	476	447
1993-1994	599	550
1994-1995	712	654
1995-1996	837	770
1996-1997	942	858
1997-1998	1038	961
1998-1999	1081	992
1999-2000	1220	1093
2000-2001	1279	1159
2001-2002	1379	1243
2002-2003	1486	1363
2003-2004	1615	1501
2004-2005	1759	1592
2005-2006	1844	1616
2006-2007	1883	1689
2007-2008	2104	1770
2008-2009	2183	1953
2009-2010	2262	2072
2010-2011	2318	2130
2011-2012	2438	2208
2012-2013	2448	2277
2013-2014	2467	2244
2014-2015	2637	2372

To compliment student enrollment by adding new scholarships and better facilities, the development area had to be rejuvenated and become more aggressive. We needed to go, see the people, and <u>ask</u>. Also, **we wanted to honor God by the magnitude of our requests.** We started a $6 million campaign, which was a difficult challenge during a turbulent first year. When the negative publicity occurs and everyone hears that the college is closing, no one wants to make a gift to a lost cause. I would see ten people and only one would respond with a gift. I fought through the rejection by believing that the next one will be a "yes." During the second year, the fall enrollment increased significantly, thereby generating some positive cash flow. In fact, with hard work, we even surpassed our campaign goal. In Colossians 3:23 it says, "And whatever you do, do it heartily, as to the Lord, and not to men." As a result, the Board approved the doubling of the goal. Although we surpassed this new goal, it is difficult to raise enough funds to equal the importance of tuition, room, and board. In addition, the key to the future of any university hinges on the growth of endowed funds. We were able to raise our endowment each year, but it still needed millions more in order to secure the future. Without a doubt, the increase in enrollment and gifts each year maintains a positive cash flow and remains an encouragement to any board and employees.

North Greenville University Endowments For Years 1990-2014

Year	Total
1990	$ 3,433,249
1991	$ 3,397,451
1992	$ 3,464,885
1993	$ 4,202,795
1994	$ 5,317,716
1995	$ 5,693,890
1996	$ 6,699,047
1997	$ 7,282,069
1998	$ 8,129,666
1999	$ 9,062,445

2000	$ 10,628,969
2001	$ 9,564,113
2002	$ 9,365,451
2003	$ 8,900,270
2004	$ 10,300,430
2005	$ 12,621,853
2006	$ 13,700,890
2007	$ 15,976,947
2008	$ 15,946,662
2009	$ 12,712,282
2010	$ 14,005,945
2011	$ 16,897,846
2012	$ 16,632,823
2013	$ 20,918,555
2014	$ 26,137,822

Cash flow increases if you can provide income from the summer activities on campus. We immediately addressed this concern by improving the availability of courses for summer school and attracting a camp program called Centrifuge, a Southern Baptist program involving at least 500 (currently over 1,000) campers between the ages of 13 and 18 each week for eight weeks. This allowed us to remain focused on Jesus Christ by providing the facilities for campers to hear about Him. These campers would have a good experience at North Greenville and might return as a student. Therefore, three positives would occur – life changing experience for Him, recruitment of students, and positive cash flow – the very best any university could have in the summer.

A year-round program (summer, fall, and spring) caused some concern of too much problem activity for the community, and we needed to earn the respect once again of our neighbors. Therefore, we started a college/community relations committee to improve communications between both parties and to try to gain the community's support. Communication problems can be a major inhibitor, and the college was at the crossroads in every way. Friends in the community were needed in order for the college to return to being the beacon of the community. We would sometimes humorously quip that God was at work in other places, but He lived at North Greenville!

In 2004, we became a university with 35 four-year academic majors and two graduate programs. With the addition of programs, more students were encouraged to stay at North Greenville University in the undergraduate program and/or graduate program. I learned that it is less expensive to retain a student than recruit one. Therefore, we established a solid retention program involving faculty, staff, and administration. Everyone realized that the budget, including salaries, depended on student enrollment. Because of the efforts by the employees, North Greenville University was able to give an increase in salaries since 1992, and in most years at least 5%.

Indeed, the good Lord has performed a tremendous miracle at North Greenville University in leading it to new heights. As of August, 2014, the university had 2,637 students studying in 40 undergraduate and six graduate programs. We had no indebtedness for the $60 million worth of facilities that have been built since 1991. With this total cost being paid, without having to borrow any funds, we can only thank the good Lord for His many blessings. **After all, the measure of life is not its duration, but its donation.** The most impressive thing about our facilities was how much they didn't cost because of the efforts of our own construction/maintenance personnel and in-kind gifts from others.

A few years ago, we had three major buildings under construction at the same time – the Chapel, Fine Arts Center, and a 68-bed Residence Hall. The total cost of the work was approximately $7 million. The major gifts for these buildings involved a significant amount of property that needed to be sold for the necessary cash flow to cover the costs. At the September Board of Trustees meeting, I informed the board of our dilemma concerning the need to sell the gifts of property in order to pay for the buildings. I made it very clear that without the property sales, we could not complete the buildings without borrowing from the bank. Although we had not borrowed any funds since 1991, they approved obtaining a loan if necessary. At the following January Board of Trustees meeting,

I gave them an update, and although we still had not borrowed any funds, it would be impossible to continue without a loan over the next few months. Somehow, we made it to the May meeting without borrowing, but I told them our cash flow would be weak through the summer, which would necessitate a loan unless we sold some of the property. We made it through the summer and another increase in enrollment generated a positive cash flow. This increase and other gifts allowed us to pay the remainder of the construction costs without having to borrow funds – another miracle from God. He covered the total cost and we still had over $1 million worth of property given for these buildings, which He did not allow us to sell. This property would be sold on His time schedule and not ours. **A good leader realizes the importance of waiting on the Lord.**

Most importantly, each year since 1991, we had over 100 people saved on our campus (in the last 10 years, at least 300 a year) and a total of 6,000 plus as of 2014. Many more accepted Jesus Christ through the ministry of our many mission teams. Each year, we would continue to be one of the leaders among all public and private colleges and universities when it comes to the number of student summer missionaries serving around the world.

As one can clearly see, North Greenville University has made it through the surviving and stabilizing stages and moved into the thriving stage. The school will continue to thrive as long as it remains focused on Jesus Christ in every program, and tries to always center on one more getting saved. Since the beginning in 1991, I have always said, "we want just one more." Every person at North Greenville must continue to pray diligently, heed His call, wash other people's feet as servant leaders, remain committed to quality education in a biblically sound, Christ-centered environment, and have a real passion for lost souls.

And Jesus said, **"I know you can't, but I can!!!"**

Chapter 3
OVERCOMING THE INEVITABLE

A short time after I became president, I went down to Columbia, South Carolina, to meet with the Administrative Committee of the Board of the South Carolina Baptist Convention, with the purpose of asking them for more financial support in addition to the current assistance through the Cooperative Program. The program is a unique method of funding state and national programs among Southern Baptist churches. (This South Carolina Baptist, Southern Baptist program provided over $1 million a year in support for our ministry.) Looking back, I could not believe how naïve I was in thinking that the convention would actually give more funds to help us survive. Unknown to me at the time, the Executive Committee of the Board had already made two recommendations: 1) the college would become an off-campus extension of nearby Furman University, which was still a South Carolina Baptist institution, or 2) the campus should be closed and sold. In addition, the Executive Committee had also formed a study committee to determine the feasibility of the school's survival.

To my dismay, and in spite of my impassioned plea for more funding to save North Greenville, the Administrative Committee made a motion to withdraw Cooperative Program funding. After realizing that my efforts were futile, I proceeded to let them know that there would be no feasibility study and we would move forward without them. It got heated and the disagreement basically got out of hand. My dad would say, we were butting heads. At that point,

I was asked to leave the room. To say the least, the lack of funding would mean our closing.

The newly elected Executive Director – Treasurer of the South Carolina Baptist Convention, Dr. Carlisle Driggers, could not support the motion, even though he acknowledged that he was not sure how in the world the school could be saved. He urged the Committee to table their motion for one year while he personally looked into the matter. (I understood that it was for six months instead of a year, but regardless, we were given more time on Dr. Driggers' action.)

Dr. Driggers pledged, "After studying and looking at it for a year, I give you my word, if we need to close that school down, I will come to you and ask you to close it down." This was his first major recommendation to the Committee as the Convention's new Executive Director – Treasurer. Then, he invited me back into the meeting and told me that the motion by the Committee had been tabled. Dr. Driggers recalled, "I could remember my mouth was dry and my heart was beating so fast." He remembered, "My palms were even sweaty." He thought, "I may be putting my whole career on the line right here."

He knew, "If I asked them to do this and North Greenville goes belly up 10 or 12 months from now for sure – and it already had one foot in the grave and one foot on a banana peel at that point – my tenure could be awfully short with the state convention, or at the least my leadership would be questioned from then on." **Whenever you see success, someone once made a courageous decision.** The board heeded his advice, tabled the original motion, and a substitute motion was adopted that gave North Greenville more time. Even until this day, that motion is still on the table. He explained that, "mainly our board backed off, took hands off, and waited to see what could happen in a year's time."

I was certainly grateful, but also committed. God did not call me to North Greenville to close it up, and He was bigger than any denomination. **At this point, I remembered that a person who wants to lead the orchestra must turn his back to the crowd. I'm convinced that life is 10% what happens to you and 90% how**

you react to it. Therefore, I set out to accomplish the seemingly impossible task of turning around North Greenville Junior College. And Jesus said, **"I know you can't, but I can!!!"**

Our financial woes continued, and any recovery depended on the bank's willingness to extend our line of credit. Many of the new hires were told that the job is yours, but I cannot guarantee a paycheck. Two of my new administrators were welcomed by me on their first day and told that I was on my way to the bank to see if they would increase our line of credit. If they chose not to do this, we would not make that month's payroll. I went to see Nap Vandiver and Mack Whittle at Carolina First Bank. I told them exactly our problem and our needs. Mack was hesitant, but Nap approved the increase on a handshake and convinced Mack that the bank needed to fully support this struggling institution. Both men were true to their word over the next months and years.

With 329 students at that time, $3 million in debt, not being able to pay bills or make payroll, buildings falling in all around, and the state convention giving up on us, I had to declare financial exigency, which allowed me to do whatever was necessary financially to save the school. In addition, I would see 10 people about giving and helping us, and nine of them would say "No way! I understand that you are broke and have spent the principal in your endowment funds (an institution should only spend the interest off the endowment, as directed by the endowment) for the wrong purposes. I understand you are going to close. I'm not giving to a school that is on the way out." Since I didn't know any better, I decided to begin a $6 million campaign at the worst time.

Behind the scenes, I also was keeping a critical eye, not to mention my pen, on expenses, by personally signing all requisition forms. I mean, literally every dime that was spent had to be thought through. What is this expense for? Can we get it for a better price? Do we really have to have it? Can we get them to bill us later for it? Even the smallest expenditures were managed this way in an effort to get spending under control.

Hence, the first task was to get the facilities in better shape to attract students, and at the same time establish a different attitude among faculty and staff members about using the college's money. We really had to create the idea that this is the Lord's money, which you do not spend unless you have a good reason and it is going to glorify the Lord.

My experiences in higher education, and my familiarity with North Greenville's past and present, allowed me to better understand as well as deal with a struggling school. I was able to train the key people on my staff on how I wanted them to perform their responsibilities, and then hold them accountable. I'd been a recruiter; I had been a fundraiser; I had worked in student services, financial aid, and athletics; and taught in the classroom. Also, from my experiences in all of these areas at North Greenville before returning as president, I knew where all the potholes and/or landmines might be and could avoid them, as well as know how to fix them. Now I can see that through all of my life experiences, God was preparing me for this task.

One must remember that I was not necessarily casting a new vision, but was, in effect, calling the school to reclaim its heritage. I wanted everyone to have a cause to rally around, so the good Lord used an unlikely request to build unity. Marion Moorhead asked for my assistance in finding a bell like the one used when the school was an Academy.

Marion Moorhead and his wife were missionaries in Japan for many, many years and he attended North Greenville when it was an Academy, as well as a Junior College. He was the President of the Academy Club. So, he asked me to come over to the First Baptist Church in Easley, South Carolina, to talk about a matter, and I was excited because I thought he was going to help me with fundraising. When I arrived at the meeting with Marion, he told me that he was the President of the Academy Club, and there were many silver-haired ladies and older men who had graduated from North Greenville Academy who wanted to see a bell like the one they had when they attended North Greenville back on our campus. He told me that they had raised about $700 or $800, and they needed a lot more to get a bell. He also wanted to know if I would help them raise money for the bell, or help them find a bell for the campus. Since the school was founded in 1892, they wanted to celebrate 100 years in September, 1992. It would be a great thing to celebrate Founder's Day with this bell on the campus. Well, to say the least, I was devastated. I patronized Marion as best I could. Then I left the church and got in my car and said, "I cannot believe that I have just been asked to find a 'blooming' bell when I am not even sure that the school will be here in another month."

As I was driving from Easley, I came to White Horse Road, and the Lord put on my heart and mind the need to turn right instead of left. Perhaps there was a bell not far up that road. And sure enough, as I turned right and drove about half a mile, there was a landscaping company with a big bell, just like the one they wanted back on the campus. I couldn't believe it. I said, "Lord, you have provided the bell. You sent me straight to it."

I pulled into the parking lot, got out and found the owner, and I said, "Sir, I'm Jimmy Epting at North Greenville College and I need that bell. We are wanting to celebrate 100 years with it. Will you let me buy it or give it to me?" He looked at me and said, "Sir, I don't care who you are, but everybody's daddy, brother, and anybody else you can think of has come by here and tried to get that bell from me, and I'm not letting it go. I am keeping that bell." I couldn't believe it. I couldn't understand why God had brought me to see that bell if He didn't want us to have it. I tried diligently to get him to change his mind, but he would not. Then I asked him, "Is there anyone else that has a bell like that?" He said, "There is a man near the hospital that makes bells. You can check with him." He told me how to get to the bell-maker's location. When I arrived at his business, I told the man about our need. He said, "Sir, I can't make a bell that big, but I can tell you another guy who has a bell like that. He lives in Fountain Inn." So, I got his number and name, but I kept checking back with the landscaping guy and he wouldn't budge.

Finally, I called the guy in Fountain Inn, and he said' "Oh, you are just a little late. This Texas tycoon has just bought that bell and he is going to be shipping it back to Texas, because he is a big bell collector." I said, "Could you give me his name and his number?" Believe it or not, he did! The next day, I called this man's office. He must have had fourteen secretaries, because that day I got one person who was way down the line. I began calling him about every other day and I kept getting a different secretary and a different person. Finally, I got to his main assistant and I said, "Ma'am, my name is Jimmy Epting and I am President at North Greenville College, and I just want to talk to your boss about this bell he has in South Carolina and about bells in general. You see, I felt like if I made him think I was going to talk to him about bells, and that was his hobby, then he would probably talk to me. Sure enough, he came on the phone and he said, "Hello there, good buddy. How you doing?" When he came across with that good ole' country tone to his voice, I had a good feeling that I had him, because that was talking my language. In the same tone, I responded, "Sir, I am so glad to talk to you about this bell you have in South Carolina, and I need for you to let me get that bell from you." He said, "Son, I've been wanting that bell. I've got a lot of other bells and I'm trying to have a good sampling of different bells from all over the nation. I just can't let you get that bell from me." And I said, "But sir, there are a lot of 70- and 80-year-old men and women who graduated from our Academy who want us to get a bell back on our campus like the bell that was at the Academy. These folks don't have long to live, and if you don't help me get this bell, they may never see this happen. You have got to let me have this bell." I gave him my best, good ole' Baptist preacher's kid talk. I learned early from my daddy how to beg. Being a Baptist preacher, he had to do a lot of begging. So finally, he said ok. "I won't ship it back to Texas. You can get the bell from me." And I said, "Sir, there is one more thing. We don't have any money and I need for you to give me that bell." Then he said, "Do what?" I said, "Yes Sir. I need that bell and I need you to give it to me, because I know the good Lord wants you to do that." He said, "Okay. I'll do it. I don't know why, but I will do it."

When I went to Fountain Inn to get the bell, the guy in Fountain Inn wouldn't give it to me. He said, "There is no way, because he went to too much trouble to buy that bell." I gave the man in Fountain Inn the number and the Texas tycoon verified that the bell was North Greenville College's bell. I got a wrecker to move it and put it in my garage at the president's house. That thing weighed two, three, or four tons, so I can't image why I put it in there. I guess I was thinking somebody might get it, but that wasn't going to happen because nobody could move it.

The next task was to get a little bell tower on our campus, because it was getting close to Founder's Day and we wanted to celebrate 100 years with that bell on campus. I called a construction company owner in Greer, South Carolina, named Buddy Waters. I didn't know him at the time, but I had heard good things about him.

I said, "Mr. Waters, I need for you and your company to build a small bell tower on our campus so I can put this bell in that tower. We want it in time to celebrate 100 years at North Greenville." Mr. Waters responded by saying, "We will be glad to help you. We love North Greenville. Now, when do you need it?" I said, "We've got to have it in a couple of weeks." He said, "What?" I said, "Yes, Sir. We've got to have it in a couple of weeks." He said, "I don't know if we can do that." I said, "I hope you can because we have got to have it." I told him the story about the celebration and those dear old men and women who need to see this bell as well as celebrate 100 years on Founder's Day.

He said, "Well, how much money do you have to pay for it?" And I said, "That's the other thing. I need you to donate your services and also the supplies and materials to make it happen." He got quiet. Then Mr. Waters said, "Are you kidding me?" I said, "No, Sir. I feel God wants you to do this. We want the Academy Club members to have one last opportunity to see that bell on this campus." Well, he said "We will try!" He brought his crew up and they built the prettiest bell tower and hung the bell in it. We got everything ready for Founder's Day except painting the white trim on the bell tower roof.

Oh, I was so excited. "Look what I had done!" Look what we had accomplished. Now we are going to have a great Founder's Day. During Founder's Day, we will have the speaker, then we will go outside, and I will let every Academy Club graduate ring the bell. We will ring it 100 times to celebrate 100 years (1892 to 1992). Guess What? That morning, on Founder's Day, 1992, it was pouring down rain. I couldn't believe it. I said, "Lord, how in the world did You let this happen? We were going to have the greatest celebration and I went to all this trouble to make it happen."

Then I thought, we will get some crazy student to go out there and ring that bell 100 times while we watch him under the cover of the porch. Sure enough, the Founder's Day speaker finished and we went outside to celebrate one hundred years. I was standing out on the porch under the cover and I turned to the dear lady beside me. She must have been at least 85. I felt as if "my buttons are about to pop off my shirt." Oh, how proud I was. Look what I have done. I looked over to her and said, "Isn't this great! We got that bell on campus and the guy is ringing it 100 times. Aren't you happy?"

I did a double take because tears were flowing down this sweet lady's face. I said, "Ma'am, are you okay?" And she said, "Oh, yes sir. I'm okay, but Dr. Epting…" she looked at me with eyes of compassion and tears flowing, "I just did not think that I would see a bell like the one we used to have on our campus again at North Greenville. For you see, the sound of the ringing of the bell and seeing that bell brings back the spirit of Jesus Christ on this campus. Oh, thank the Lord. Thank the Lord that the spirit is back."

I thought a minute and then I said, "Oh Lord, please forgive me. This was all about me and how proud I was for getting this bell on this campus, and you have let me see very clearly now that it's all about You. And if we are going to keep the Spirit of Jesus Christ on this campus, and allow You to make a difference on this campus, then it's got to be totally and completely about You, dear Lord, not about any of us, and especially not about Jimmy Epting."

Tom White, a 1952 graduate, expressed it this way: "North Greenville's walls are not ivory nor are her streets of gold, but her spirit is that of consuming love. Her power lies not in her possessing strange or unique gifts but in her willingness to seek and be receptive to such gifts. Her struggle to survive has not dimmed her light but has made her more brilliant where darkness prevails. Her being cannot decline, for her foundation is not perishable quality – her foundation was laid by hands of those seeking to have the ways of God initiated in human lives. Her spirit is written in the hearts of men.

However it may come, the Spirit is present. It rises from those walls as surely as the mist rises from the surrounding hills. And as surely as the mist is scattered by the climbing sun, the North Greenville spirit is scattered wherever the school's graduates have gone, for it lives in the hearts of those who have known and loved North Greenville."

Yes, the spirit permeates all things on our campus, and we have only begun. The ultimate goal was and hopefully still is for all South Carolina Baptists to say without hesitation, if you're planning to go into full-time Christian service, then North Greenville College is where you need to continue your education.

No longer just a lighthouse of the dark corner, but a lighthouse of Christian education for all South Carolina and the world.

To help with this reclaiming of our heritage, I wanted to enhance it with a new logo and/or seal or emblem being seen all over our campus, as well as on pins worn by our employees, which stated that, "Christ Makes the Difference." It conveys the tradition, history, and purpose of North Greenville University. Psalm 43:3 says, "Oh, send out your light and your truth! Let them lead me; Let them bring me to Your holy hill, and to Your tabernacle." The book in the logo indicates commitment to pursuing truth in academics and through studying God's word; the flame represents God's light and the pursuit of truth. Obviously, the cross is where Jesus shed His blood for you and me.

The key is to be committed to Christ making the difference. We definitely did not want to be like a kamikaze pilot who went on 16 missions. He was only involved and not committed. From day one, I believed North Greenville could be true to this commitment. It has been reported that the flying Wallendas decided to cross Niagara Falls, so they stretched a cable and walked across it. Then, one of the cable walkers asked, "Who thinks I can walk the cable while pushing a wheelbarrow?" One scrawny kid was so excited and screamed, "I know you can!" Then the cable walker said, "If you believe I can do it so much, get in the barrow." **Believing – it goes from the head to the heart.**

On my knees the first day as president, it went from my head to my heart when Jesus said, **"I know you can't, but I can!!!"**

Chapter 4
CALLED TO SERVE

A leader needs to focus on what he or she has, and what they make of it. In the 80s, when I served as vice president at North Greenville, we lived about a mile from the college and we had enough land for a vegetable garden. It was located across the street from Mrs. Ward's house. Now Mrs. Ward had a huge garden in her backyard, at least two acres, and she had two green thumbs. She forgot more about gardening than I ever knew about it. Since she was up in age and needed to use a walker, she had what I call a chair garden. She would enter her garden at the break of light and be through working it by the time I left for work. Every 100 feet she had a chair placed strategically so she could hoe a row and sit to rest when needed.

She tried to teach me the right way to garden, and enjoyed watching me when I arrived home in the evening to work in my garden. She would rock in her chair and enjoy two things – my gardening efforts and her snuff. I knew I was in trouble when I heard her spit the snuff so hard that it made a ringing sound when it hit the spittoon. Then, she would holler, "Jimmy, if you don't put a string over the top of your beans, the crows are going to eat them; and if you don't hoe around the corn better, it will not grow properly; and…." It would continue until I would reach the point of exasperation and want to tell Mrs. Ward to "put this hoe where the sun don't shine," but I didn't.

She just wanted me to stop and rock with her on her porch. When I spent time with her, she would always say, "Jimmy, when you become president of North Greenville College, I want you to share my favorite story with the students." If she told me once, she told it to me dozens of times. It was not her story, and I'm not sure where it came from, but she claimed it. She didn't live to see me become president. One day I got an emergency call to come quickly, for she was having a serious problem. When I entered the house, Mrs. Ward was lying on the bathroom floor and close to death. Her relative and I tried to resuscitate her to no avail. As I was pushing on her heart, I felt the Spirit of the Lord in the room. It was as if an angel was pushing me back and ready to take Mrs. Ward to Glory land. But I have never forgotten her or "her story," which I did share with our new students on their first day at North Greenville University every year.

In ancient times there was a wise man and a prince, and all the people in the colony loved the wise man. He would go down to the marketplace every day and see the people, hug on them, listen to them, care about their needs, and basically love all of them. The prince was jealous, because all the people loved the wise man. He did not understand, because he was supposed to be the main guy in the colony. He just did not have time to reach out to the people. (At this point in telling her story, I would talk to the students about making a difference by reaching out to others and caring, as well as doing many of the same things as the wise man.)

Well, the prince came up with a plan. He told the few followers he had around him that he would disguise himself as a peasant, go down to the marketplace, and get everybody's attention. He would have in his hands a white dove, and he would ask the wise man if the dove was dead or alive. If he says that it's dead, I'll let it fly away and flourish; and if he says that it's alive, I will crush it and let it fall to the ground. The wise man will not know the answer and he will look like a fool. The people will not like him and they will like me, the prince. True to his word, the prince got his few followers, disguised himself as a peasant, and went down to the marketplace to confront the wise man.

When he got everyone's attention, the prince asked the wise man whether the dove in his hands was dead or alive. The wise man looked at the prince, disguised as a peasant, with eyes of compassion, and said, "Oh son, you just do not understand; that which you have in your hands is what you make of it. It is indeed what you do with what you have."

Mrs. Ward's story helped the new students understand that the educational experience and their success is what they make of it. It is indeed what you do with what you have. In addition, in serving as the leader, her story provides me with the same advice.

On our campus there are three sculptures that give physical and spiritual reminders of what it takes to be a servant leader, which plays a vital role in our commitment to quality education in a biblically sound, Christ-centered environment. The first sculpture is based on Matthew 4:18-20 and is called **Fishers of Men.** The sculpture is life-sized, and has Jesus holding a fishnet.

These verses tell us that Jesus is walking along the shore of Galilee when He says to Peter and Andrew, "Follow me, and I will make you fishers of men. They immediately left their nets and followed him." They did not ask anyone for permission and there was no hesitation. They were obedient to the call.

I like to think that God called and I followed. Looking back, although I did not move immediately and did not believe I was capable nor smart enough for such an awesome responsibility, I did make myself available. **It always comes down to your availability and your desire to let it be about God's glory. Our purpose is not to have and hold, but to give and serve. The service we render to others is really the rent we pay for our room on earth. I realized a long time ago that if you want true happiness, be in God's will.**

Further, we want our students to drop their nets and follow Jesus. It does not necessarily mean that every student will go directly into some kind of ministry. Remember, we believe at North Greenville University that all vocations need to be Christian vocations and thus, all are called to be fishers of men.

When I think of a servant leader, I am reminded of John the Baptist, because he clearly understood his role and purpose. He was obedient to God's call. There is no way to get around it – John was very unique. He began preaching in the Judean wilderness and his message was that men must turn from their sins and to God because the kingdom of heaven was near. You must understand that after the death of Elijah, the voice of God's prophets would be silent for 400 years. The Jewish leaders had been waiting for the Messiah, Elijah, or a prophet. John declared in the words of Isaiah, "I am a voice of one crying in the wilderness: 'Prepare the way of the Lord; Make His paths straight.'" (Matthew 3:3). John the Baptist was not a resurrected Elijah, but he took on Elijah's prophetic role in fulfillment of the Old Testament Scriptures. Also, John's clothes were woven from camel's hair, he wore a leather belt, and his food was locusts and wild honey.

Let's stop right here and put this in proper perspective. I am not impressed with this locust diet. I have a garden, and one of the vegetables that is not hard to grow is green beans. I did not realize this fact when growing up as a Baptist pastor's kid. In the summer, church members would bring us green beans every day. I thought it was special until I realized how easy it is to grow them. Anyway, I got tired of green beans every meal and mom always had some honey on the table. When she was not looking, I would pour honey on the green beans. When you put honey on anything, all you taste is the honey. Therefore, I'm not impressed with John the Baptist eating honey and locusts, but I am impressed with his humility.

In John 3:30, John the Baptist said, "He (Jesus Christ) must increase, but I must decrease." Also, he said in John 1:29-30, "Behold, the Lamb of God who takes away the sin of the world! This is He of whom I said, 'After me comes a Man who is preferred before me, for He was before me.'" He continued in Mark 1:7, "There comes One after me who is mightier than I, whose sandal strap I'm not worthy to stoop down and loose." John the Baptist was "the man" and had hundreds coming to the Jordan River to be baptized. They were following him. But he knew his role, and that he was **called to serve**. His calling was to prepare the way for Jesus Christ.

In trying to serve Jesus Christ at North Greenville University, and from John the Baptist's example, I realized that I must work harder for it to be about Jesus and not me. Some years ago, the student music group 'Joyful Sound' and I were invited to be at the First Baptist Church in Spartanburg, South Carolina, which meant we were going to be on T.V. I had never been on T.V., and to say the least, I was excited about this opportunity. I called my mom and told her the good news, and immediately she informed me that she was not going to miss her church in order to see me on T.V. (a good Baptist preacher's wife – probably worried about what the deacons might say). I told her not to worry about it, because we would tape it and she could see it later.

When we left the campus for Spartanburg, it was raining and quite stormy. We arrived early for the first service at 8:30 am, and all went well. But the service that would be on T.V. was at 11:00 am, and my moment of stardom would be soon. Between the services, they showed me around the facilities, talked about the next service, and showed me the clock at the front, which indicated that the Spirit stops moving at 12 noon; or maybe that was when the service ended on T.V. Then, we went to a room in the back of the church to have prayer with the deacons. After prayer time, we proceeded to the door that led to the sanctuary, and as we entered at 11:00 am, the place went totally black. The storm had gotten worse and knocked out all the power.

Oh no! Surely this was not happening to me, since this was my first opportunity to be on T.V. All of a sudden, I thought of John 3:30, "He (Jesus) must increase, but I must decrease." I had been thinking it was all about me. At that moment, I made it right with God and we had a good service in the dark. Jesus Christ showed out in spite of me. By the way, I do not believe a power outage had ever happened before or since that day.

Over the years at North Greenville University, we have tried to have Jesus Christ increase and make the difference. I believe that our efforts have not gone unnoticed, but have actually been rewarded. You may recall that Jesus said in Matthew 11:11, "Assuredly, I say to you, among those born of women there has not risen one greater than John the Baptist; but he who is least in the kingdom of heaven is greater than he."

The second sculpture on campus is based on John 13, and is called **Divine Servant.** The life-sized sculpture depicts Jesus on his knees washing a disciple's feet. Starting with verse four, it says that Jesus, "rose from supper and laid aside His garments, took a towel and girded Himself. After that, He poured water into a basin and began to wash the disciples' feet, and to wipe them with the towel with which He was girded."

Then, in verse 14 Jesus said, "If I then, your Lord and Teacher, have washed your feet, you also ought to wash one another's feet." This sculpture is located in front of our Ministry/Welcome Center, at the top of the first hill as you come through the main entrance. Every day, when I entered the campus, I would see the sculpture, which reminded me as president, but more importantly as a Christian, that I was to wash someone's feet. Jesus set the best leadership example of all, and if I have been **called to serve**, I need to be more like Christ in all that I say and do in my role as a servant leader. **I must make service my first priority, not success; and success will follow!**

In front of the main Administration Building in the middle of campus, located between the Chapel and Fine Arts Building, we have our third sculpture called **Gethsemane**. It is based on Matthew 26:36. It is a life-sized sculpture of Jesus praying after He told his disciples, "Sit here while I go and pray over there." It is clear that prayer is the key to our success in the past and for the future. No decision was made at North Greenville University without first praying about it and seeking God's will. Our faculty and staff knew that every decision I made was bathed in prayer. If I made a bad decision, it was because I did what I wanted, and not what God wanted. Unfortunately, I did not always understand God's plan, but everyone was assured that I tried my best to follow His will. **Whenever you see a successful leader, you know that someone made a courageous decision based on prayer.**

In order to be an effective leader, I needed to understand that I do not pray to inform God of what is happening. He already knows. I do not pray to get Him to do what I want. He already wants what is best for everyone involved. I pray to maintain a right relationship with God.

Jesus taught us to lead creatively and wisely, but He refused to tell us exactly how to do it. He just said that the Word of God must be our truth, and that He would leave His Spirit to guide ours. He also told us to pray.

By answering the call to lead, I committed myself to enable others to see their dream more clearly and somehow make it happen. That is spiritual business and it cannot be done well without effective communication with the Spirit of God through prayer. When I lead well, exceptional achievement is possible. That is why I answered the call to lead. It is also why people follow great leaders. And, it is why leaders pray so fervently.

But don't be fooled by this; if leadership were easy, everyone would be a great leader. Great leadership is from the Spirit. The life of the Spirit may be simple, even obvious, but it is never easy.

And Jesus said, **"I know you can't, but I can!!!"**

Chapter 5
RENEWING THE PASSION

Some of my strategies for reversing the downward trend at North Greenville and implementing the turnaround were a new institutional mission, the development and improvement of academic programs that broadened the constituency, a fresh image of the institution, an update of student expectations, a transformational leadership style, an aggressive fund-raising campaign, the promotion of the institution's core values, and the creation of a strategic plan for institutional advancement. And, most importantly, being passionate about all the above.

I realized then, and over the years, that getting the right teaching faculty was important to achieve our mission, and from day one I began to personally interview everyone who worked here. During the interview, I asked if the person was a Christian and invited them to tell me about their salvation experience. Also, I asked about their service for Jesus Christ in the church and community. Then, we discussed their passion about sharing Jesus Christ with others. In 1991, many employees did not agree with our mission and did not want to be a part of it. I dismissed several people, although some of the dismissals led to sharp criticism and even lawsuits. Even if they were good people, who loved the Lord, and were great teachers, but were unwilling to be true to the mission of the school and be loyal to the board and me, then they needed to go.

In my eyes, this was a key step to later success. You are only as good as your people. It was imperative to find good people, but I had to find people who would work for less, who were willing to work hard, who realized there was hope, and who could visualize that there was a future. They had to have real passion about their ministry at North Greenville.

I'm reminded of a story about a farmer, a preacher, and a garden. You see, the farmer had a lot that was filled with rocks and weeds, and was in really bad shape. He decided it was time to clean it up and perhaps plant a garden. So, he went to work - he cleaned up the property, cultivated it, and then he planted his garden. Oh, what a beautiful garden! He had worked so hard in that garden! The plants had grown and it was time to pick the vegetables. He worked hard that morning hoeing it out and being sure that it was fertilized again and properly watered. It was time that afternoon to pick. He did his picking and had a good harvest of green beans, corn, tomatoes, and okra. Then, he sat under a tree because he was just worn out.

About that time, like any Baptist would do, the minister timed it perfectly and came over and said, "Mr. Farmer sir, my goodness! That is a tremendous garden, sir; and look at all that you have been able to pick. I'll tell you what, you should be very proud of that garden and how things look." The old farmer was sitting under that shade tree with perspiration flowing down his face. He was soaking wet from working so hard. The pastor continued, "I know that the good Lord sure has blessed you with this garden. I know that's what you are thinking. How much the good Lord has blessed you in this garden." And the farmer replied, "Well, no. I guess that's true; but really, what I was thinking was you should have seen this place when the good Lord had it by Himself."

The farmer wasn't trying to be disrespectful to our Lord and Savior, but he was making it clear to the pastor that the good Lord expects us to do our part. And, He expects us to have real passion when it comes to working hard and making things look nice. That old farmer knew the good Lord could do it by Himself, but He gave the farmer the ability to work hard and make it happen. With God all things are possible!

Another key strategy of the revitalization process was to make sure those who were hired or moved up were supportive of our mission. The primary concerns were that all employees be Christian; believe in the mission of the school, and support God's chosen leader. Any good leader needs to be allowed to surround himself/herself with the people who can best help him/her accomplish his/

her objectives, build upon his/her strengths, and alleviate his/her weaknesses.

In time, as many people began to sense that I was only trying to do what I sincerely believed God wanted, the faculty and staff started to realize that I was not as bad as everybody claimed before I arrived. When I was observed working day and night to improve the buildings, find new donors and raise funding, recruit students, and ensure the school's survival (even though it meant making tough decisions), they began to accept me and gradually, trust developed. But I had to make the right decisions. Our employees had to see progress, growth, and good things happening.

The greatest regret I have is concerning my family. For the first two to three years, my wife had to raise our children because my family was a distant third on my priority list – God, North Greenville, and family. I did not join them for any vacations during this time and seldom spent a day without doing something for the University. The family finally accepted the fact that I would recruit students everywhere I went - at restaurants, theaters, and churches. Also, I would try to raise friends and funds from every human contact. They were embarrassed early on, but they finally got used to it.

At the same time, **I wanted to be judged by others on how I treat those who I think can do nothing for me.** You can easily judge the character of others by how they treat those who they think can do nothing for them.

> **"People will forget what you said, people will forget what you did, but people will never forget how you made them feel."** – Maya Angelou

So as president of North Greenville, I knew that in everything I was to say and do, I had to be a genuine, caring, loving person.

Looking at the school's past enabled me to discover its real strength. This school was known for strong training of those who go into full-time ministry. We can build on this. The school was sending mixed signals before I arrived, because the school had lost its focus and passion. In addition to renewing the commitment to be a strong South Carolina Baptist institution, we desired to feature a

Christ-centered experience, provide a biblically sound educational environment, and offer a strong academic curriculum.

Most importantly, we wanted North Greenville to be known as "a place where Christ makes the difference." Even today, this slogan is bold because so many institutions do not want to talk about Jesus Christ and do not want Jesus mentioned. We put our slogan and emblem on everything. A donor helped the school purchase chimes that played Christian music on campus. We required students to attend chapel twice each week, encouraged faculty members to have prayer and devotion before starting classes, and integrated faith into everything from athletic events to academic programs.

From the beginning, we began communicating that we wanted one more saved. We realized that if we are going to grow, we're going to grow with lost people. So, we decided we wanted both non-Christian and Christian students. While all students are expected to sign a conduct agreement stating their intent to abide by normative Christian values, they do not have to be Christian to attend North Greenville, because we want to reach out and really make a difference in their lives. Our passion for everyone is: get saved, get stronger in your walk, and graduate. Our passion corresponded with our mission statement.

Observing that many other educational institutions have moved away from their religious heritage and moorings in the name of academic freedom, I believe that this tenet is precisely what makes North Greenville so unique. When you become unique, you have something to sell, market, promote, and develop. A key element was creating an environment where Christian parents would want to send their children. We felt like it was important to be conservative in our beliefs, be passionate about Jesus Christ in our academic world, and also be sure we were conservative in our rules and regulations, in order to promote the kind of morals and values that one needs to be true to Jesus. North Greenville needed to be the very best academic institution possible, regarding quality education in a biblically sound, Christ-centered environment.

I wanted it to be the best evangelical school. I wanted it to be the best at getting people saved on and off our campus. I wanted it to be the number one school for evangelism, the number one school for missions, and the number one school for quality education. One of the first steps in providing a quality education for our students was to require that anyone who taught full-time in its new four-year program hold a doctorate degree and then hold them accountable. Again, passion is the key. We needed to renew our passion.

When I was growing up in a Baptist preacher's home, my mother was very passionate about her son being in church. Every Sunday morning, my mother would start at 7:45 am, and every fifteen minutes she would call for me to get up. Now you have to understand that my mother was a very small lady, but she had the squeakiest voice. It wasn't a loud, boisterous kind of voice. It was a squeaky, like fingernails on a blackboard kind of voice, and when she would call for me to get up, she would say it with a smile.

It would go something like this, "Jimmy, it's time to get up" - squeaky and smiley. Her voice haunts me to this day. My mother was passionate about me going to church. Churches used to hold two-week revivals. The people in most churches today would rebel. The Spirit only starts on Sunday and stops moving on Wednesday. But mother made me go every night of revival for two weeks. I would say to my mother, "The deacon kids do not have to go. Why do I have to go?" "Well you're the Baptist preacher's kid," said mother.

We always lived right beside the church in the pastorium, which I often called the sanitarium, because the deacons would always check it out on a monthly basis to see if I messed the house up. I put mom and dad in a tough situation because their little boy would always cause problems. It would aggravate the deacons and, in turn, cause concerns for mom and dad. It would only take me about three minutes to get from the pastorium to the church. Mother, why did you have to start so early? I can understand why you had to start a little bit early, but not 7:45 am – two hours ahead of time.

When I went off to college, I went three hours away from home and finally, I could miss church on Sunday. I was going to take a free cut. Now I know most of the people in Baptist circles, especially pastors, do not allow free cuts; but I was going to take a free cut for the first time in my life. I stayed up late so I could sleep later the next morning. I locked the door to my room. I took the phone off the hook so mother couldn't call me. I knew she wasn't going to miss church. I knew she wasn't going to travel three hours to be sure that I was up.

That next morning at 7:45 am, I heard that squeaky, smiley voice again. And it said, "Jimmy, it's time to get up." I said, "Oh, she's not here. Surely, she's not here." And she wasn't there; but after you have heard it for 18 years of your life and probably another nine months in the womb, you can't help but hear it the rest of your life. Even to this day, I hear my mother saying at 7:45 am every Sunday morning, in a very squeaky, smiley voice, "Jimmy, it's time to get up." She had passion!

I knew when I took the job as president, the key was not only being committed but being passionate. As stated earlier, Luke 10:27 helped me better understand. "You shall love the Lord your God with all your heart, with all your soul, with all your strength, and with all your mind…" But, when it went on to say, "and your neighbor as yourself," I realized that I must have the passion for lost souls. The best way to love somebody else is to give them Jesus. I realized that I was not sharing Jesus like I should. I wasn't taking the opportunities that were brought my way to share Him with others. If I was going to have the awesome responsibility of being the president of a Christ-centered institution, I would have to be passionate about getting one more saved. And I had to allow God to use North Greenville and me to make that happen.

> A mother had a son who was playing at the beach, and he became dirtier and dirtier by the minute. He was playing with a group of boys in the sand on the beach. The mother was watching him, but she cried out in mock distress and said, "Has anybody seen my Jimmy? I know none of these boys is my Jimmy. Has anybody seen my Jimmy?" "Mommy, mommy, mommy," shouted a voice from underneath a pile of sand. "Here I am!" Jimmy cried out. "Here I am, mommy! Here I am!"

There comes a time in our lives when we call out, "Here I am Lord! Here I am!" And with real passion, Jesus says, "Son, I see you. I know who you are. No matter how dirty you are, no matter how tough things are, no matter what's going on, I passionately love you and care for you." Just like the little boy crying out to his mommy, there comes a time when we cry out to God. "God, I'm not worthy. I'm filthy." But no matter how dirty I get, He loves me, regardless. Knowing God loves me gives me a passion to share His love with others. **The passion to share God's love was the key to our success!**

Billy Graham exhibited a lot of passion in everything he would do in his ministry. I am reminded of this heart-warming story called "The Billy Graham Suit" and it goes like this:

> *Billy Graham had been invited to a luncheon in his honor and he hesitated to accept the invitation because he was struggling with Parkinson's disease. The Charlotte leaders where the luncheon was to be held said, "We don't expect a major address. Just come and let us honor you." So, he agreed.*
>
> *After wonderful things were said about him, Dr. Graham stepped to the rostrum, looked at the crowd, and said, "I'm reminded of Albert Einstein, the great physicist. Einstein was once traveling from Princeton on a train when the conductor came down the aisle, punching the tickets of every passenger. When he came to Einstein, Einstein reached in his vest pocket. He couldn't find his ticket, so he reached in his trouser pockets. It wasn't there. He looked in his briefcase but couldn't find it. Then he looked in the seat beside him. He still couldn't find it.*
>
> *"The conductor said, 'Dr. Einstein, I know who you are. We all know who you are. I'm sure you bought a ticket. Don't worry about it.'*
>
> *"Einstein nodded appreciatively. The conductor continued down the aisle punching tickets. As he was ready to move to the next car, he turned around and saw the great physicist down on his hands and knees looking under his seat for his ticket.*

"The conductor rushed back and said, 'Dr. Einstein, Dr. Einstein, don't worry, I know who you are, no problem. You don't need a ticket. I'm sure you bought one.' Einstein looked at him and said, 'Young man, I too, know who I am. What I don't know is where I'm going.'" Having said that, Billy Graham continued,

"See the suit I'm wearing? It's a brand-new suit. My children and my grandchildren are telling me I've gotten a little slovenly in my old age. I used to be a bit more fastidious. So, I went out and bought a new suit for this luncheon and one more occasion. You know what that occasion is? This is the suit in which I'll be buried. But when you hear I'm dead, I don't want you to immediately remember the suit I'm wearing. I want you to remember this: I not only know who I am. I also know where I'm going."

The key to passion for us at North Greenville was to be sure we exhibited our passion in such a way that students in particular know exactly where they are going.

It was indeed the time to renew our passion if Jesus Christ was going to make the difference at North Greenville University. This wonderful story of a mother and her son captures the true meaning of passion.

It was one of the hottest days of the dry season. We had not seen rain in almost a month. The crops were dying. Cows had stopped giving milk. The creeks and streams were long gone back into the earth. It was a dry season that would bankrupt several farmers before it was through.

Every day, my husband and his brothers would go about the arduous process of trying to get water to the fields. Lately the process had involved taking a truck to the local water plant and filling it up with water. But severe rationing had cut everyone off. If we didn't see some rain soon, we would lose everything. It was on this day that I learned the true lesson of sharing and witnessed the only miracle I have seen with my own eyes.

I was in the kitchen making lunch for my husband and his brothers when I saw my six-year-old son, Billy, walking toward the woods. He wasn't walking with the usual carefree abandon of a youth, but with a serious purpose. I could only see his back. He was obviously walking with great effort…trying to be as still as possible. Minutes after he disappeared into the woods, he came running out again, toward the house. I went back to making sandwiches, thinking that whatever task he had been doing was completed. Moments later, he was once again walking in that slow purposeful stride toward the woods. This activity went on for an hour: walking carefully to the woods, running back to the house.

Finally, I couldn't take it any longer, so I crept out of the house and followed him on his journey (being very careful not to be seen…as he was obviously doing important work and didn't need his Mommy checking up on him). He was cupping both hands in front of him as he walked, being very careful not to spill the water he held in them… maybe two or three tablespoons were held in his tiny hands. I sneaked close as he went into the woods. Branches and thorns slapped his little face, but he did not try to avoid them. He had a much higher purpose. As I leaned in to spy on him, I saw the most amazing sight.

Several large deer loomed in front of him. Billy walked right up to them. I almost screamed for him to get away. A huge buck with elaborate antlers was dangerously close. But the buck did not threaten him…he didn't even move as Billy knelt down. And I saw a tiny fawn lying on the ground, obviously suffering from dehydration and heat exhaustion, lift its head with great effort to lap up the water cupped in my beautiful boy's hands. When the water was gone, Billy jumped up to run back to the house and I hid behind a tree.

I followed him back to the house to a spigot, to which we had shut off the water. Billy opened it all the way up and a small trickle began to creep out. He knelt there, letting the drip slowly fill up his makeshift "cup," as the sun beat down on his little back. And it came clear to me: The trouble he had gotten into for playing with the hose the week before. The lecture he had received about the importance of not wasting water. The reason he didn't ask me to help him. It took almost twenty minutes for the drops to fill his hands. When he stood up and began the trek back, I was there in front of him.

His little eyes just filled with tears. "I'm not wasting," was all he said. As he began his walk, I joined him…with a small pot of water from the kitchen. I let him tend to the fawn. I stayed away. It was his job. I stood on the edge of the woods watching the most beautiful heart I have ever known working so hard to save another life. As the tears that rolled down my face began to hit the ground, other drops…and more drops…and more, suddenly joined them. I looked up at the sky. It was as if God, himself, was weeping with pride.

Some will probably say that this was all just a huge coincidence. Those miracles don't really exist. That it was bound to rain sometime. And I can't argue with that…I'm not going to try. All I can say is, the rain that came that day saved our farm…just like the actions of one little boy saved another.

I don't know if anyone will read this…but I had to send it out. To honor the memory of my beautiful Billy, who was taken from me much too soon. But not before showing me the true face of God, in a little, sunburned boy.

Now, that's God! That's God! A real passion of a little boy to love another, to give to another. God is in the miracle business. North Greenville University is a miracle, and in the business to love and give life to others. And Jesus said, **"I know you can't, but I can!!!"**

Chapter 6
TEAMWORK AND CHANGE

The old city slicker was driving his car out in the country one day and he wasn't paying attention to the curve in the road. He lost control of the car and it went into the ditch. He was basically out in the middle of nowhere and he couldn't get the car out of the ditch. Up just a little way from where he got his car stuck was a farmer sitting on the porch at his house.

The city slicker walked up to the farm and said, "Farmer, I guess you can see that my car is in the ditch down here. Is there anything that you can do to help me get it out?" The old farmer said, "No, I don't think there is much I can do to help you." The old city slicker said, "You have got to be able to do something to help. I have got to get my car out. I've got to get back home. Isn't there anything that you can do?" The farmer said, "Well, I've got the old mule out there. He is blind as he can be. He can't see a lick. His name is Dusty. I guess I could try to hook Dusty up to your car and see if he can pull the car out, but it's a stretch for him to do it."

Well the man said, "I appreciate you at least trying to help. If you can just make an effort with Dusty, that would be saying something for us, and maybe it could work. Even though, I don't know how one mule is going to pull that car out of the ditch." The farmer slowly moved to the barn, got his harnesses and everything he needed to hook that old blind mule, Dusty, to the car. He had a whip in his hand. He got everything just perfectly set up and he popped that whip and he hollered "Pull, Bill!" And of course, nothing happened. He popped that whip again and said "Pull, Jack!" Still nothing happened. He popped that whip again and said "Pull, Dusty!" Old Dusty started pulling and pulling, and pulled just enough to get that car out of the ditch.

Oh, the old city slicker profusely thanked that farmer. He couldn't say enough wonderful things about the old mule. Finally, he stopped and said, "Farmer, I have just got to ask you, why did you holler out 'Pull, Bill,' and 'Pull, Jack' before you said, 'Pull, Dusty?'" The old farmer looked at the old boy and said, "Well, I told you that Dusty couldn't see a lick, he's blind. I did it that way because you didn't think Dusty could do it by himself, did you?" The point of the story is that Dusty thought he had two more helping him, that he had a team, and that team would make the difference because they would work well together.

From day one I have tried to encourage all members of our administrative team to become deeply involved in a sense of purpose and commitment. **A team functioning at their optimum becomes more group goal-oriented and less centered on the individual. Why do teams with less talent defeat more talented teams? TEAMWORK.** What happened at North Greenville could be summed up in the following statement: **Most things wrong in our lives started with neglecting what is right.** North Greenville had drifted and perhaps not even realized it. It would take solid teamwork to turn us around and move us forward. One can get on a float at the dock on the lake with the water being completely calm, and if you fall asleep for a few minutes, you can wake up and realize you have drifted quite a distance from the dock.

When I showed up as president, it became clear that many faculty and staff felt that North Greenville, even though a struggling institution, was still committed to providing a Christian education. It came down to the saying, **"What you do speaks so loudly, I cannot hear what you have to say."** The communication internally and externally about the school's plight was either purposefully misleading or not wanting to state the obvious by being realistic about the present and future.

Effectively communicating the vision engages, empowers, and energizes others to invest themselves in achieving more together as a team than they previously thought possible. Also, I understood the value of employing and equipping skilled and knowledgeable personnel, and fostering teamwork. I wanted the team to accept my vision to be the most affordable, private, accredited, Christ-centered, four-year university in the Southeast, while keeping Christ as the head and center of all our thinking and conduct. To never drift from it, adequately communicate it, and with teamwork, strengthen it.

With teamwork comes change, and North Greenville has certainly experienced its share of change. Today, technology keeps changing and just as I'm trying to get used to email, all kinds of other communications through computers, iPhones, and other devices are popping up.

I am reminded of the story about a man who went down to Florida, and his wife was to come the next day. He sent her an email and got the wrong address, much like I would do. His email went to a new widow. Her husband, a Baptist minister, had just died, and she checked her e-mail after the funeral. She saw this man's email and she fainted. When her son came in to see what was wrong, he checked on her to see if she was well. He glanced at the screen and it read, "To my lovely wife, I checked in and all is well – I am looking forward to you coming tomorrow. Your name is on the registry, so everything is set for you to come." P.S.: – "It is awfully hot down here, so dress light. Love, your husband."

Looking back over the years since the founding of North Greenville Academy in 1892, I see some things that have changed, but some that have not. Hugh Lafayette Brock, principal from 1893–1895, opened the school on January 16, 1893, and said, "Educating the young is second only to preaching the gospel." "Like the work of the gospel," he said, "True education prepares the heart as well as the mind both for time and for eternity. It is far more important to plant principles of truth and right in the heart than mere intelligence in the mind. Implant both together and well-rounded character is the result."

J. H. Barton, Sr. said, when the school was founded, "Eternity alone will reveal the good the school will do."

North Greenville University has strived to be true to the above by being committed to quality education in a biblically sound,

Christ-centered environment. Dr. Claude Donnan, when he became principal in 1928, said, "Without making a study of the facts as to the future of North Greenville, I accepted the place, believing and trusting that the Lord was leading. The outlook for new students for the fall session was poor." He reported to E. B. Crain, Chairman of the Board of Trustees, "That everywhere I went, the people were inquiring if the Academy would open in the fall." Crain replied, "Brother Donnan, don't let that bother you. The school has been dying ever since I knew it." Crain also said, "In overcoming the power of darkness, North Greenville has done more good than all the revenue officers and sheriffs combined for a hundred years. In instilling a love for Christ, it has changed the streams once used for whiskey into rivers of baptism."

We wanted the kind of teamwork and change that made it clear – North Greenville University is no longer just a lighthouse in the dark corner of Greenville County, but a lighthouse of Christ-centered education for all the world.

But change must occur in one's heart before it can affect the team, its work, and eventually an institution. In Mark 10:43, it says, "Whoever desires to become great among you shall be your servant." As a Christian servant, God must be prevalent through your actions after you have a genuine relationship with Him. Each member of the team must see himself/herself as a servant with a strong relationship with Jesus Christ. Then, the team is able to make a difference. The main goal of our teamwork at North Greenville was one more getting saved, "Just one more." We wanted to make a difference, one at a time.

> *Once upon a time there was a wise man who used to go to the ocean to do his writing. He had a habit of walking on the beach before he began his work. One day he was walking along the shore. As he looked down the beach, he saw a human figure moving like a dancer. He smiled to himself to think of someone who would dance to the day. So, he began to walk faster to catch up. As he got closer, he saw that it was a young man and the young man wasn't dancing. Instead he was reaching down to the*

shore, picking up something, and very gently throwing it into the ocean.

As he got closer, he called out, "Good morning! What are you doing?" The young man paused, looked up and replied, "Throwing starfish in the ocean." "I guess I should have asked, 'Why are you throwing starfish into the ocean?" The young man said, "The sun is up, the tide is going out, and if I don't throw them in, they'll die."

"But, young man, don't you realize that there are miles and miles of beach, and starfish all along it. You can't possibly make a difference!" The young man listened politely. Then he bent down, picked up another starfish, and threw it into the sea past the breaking waves, and said, "It made a difference for that one."

At North Greenville University it was always about "one more" through strong teamwork.

In 2 Chronicles 25:1, it says that "Amaziah was 25 years old when he became king, and he reigned 29 years in Jerusalem." In verse 2 it says, "He did what was right in the eyes of the Lord, but not with a loyal heart." It was very clear that change through teamwork was what it would take for North Greenville to move forward. That's what had to happen in my presidency as the leader of the team. I had to be sure that I was not like Amaziah; that I did what was right and I did it with my whole heart. I have to admit that along the way, I haven't always done that. I'm as guilty as the next person.

Let me give you an example of a time when I was definitely guilty. I had many opportunities to go and speak almost every Sunday. I had been going Sunday after Sunday after Sunday, and on this particular Saturday I was just worn out. I checked my calendar and I was to be at Nazareth Baptist Church in Blacksburg, South Carolina, which was about an hour to an hour and a half from North Greenville. I thought, "I'm tired and that is such a small church. Blacksburg is a small town. Gee, why did I agree to take that opportunity?" I was not excited about it at all.

I said, "I might as well make the best of it." Therefore, I called my son, Bert, who was attending a school that was not far from there, and I said, "Son, why don't you come to Blacksburg at Nazareth Baptist Church? It is not far from where you are going to school. Why don't you come over and hear me preach and be a part of that service?" The first thing he said was, "Dad, I don't know. I've already heard you." I said, "That's funny, Son," but I thought about it and said, "Why don't you bring some of your buddies and I will feed you." Still he said, "I don't know, but we'll think about it, Dad." (I knew that college kids would come if you feed them.)

The next morning, I headed for Blacksburg. I kept begrudging the opportunity and had a pity party with the Lord. I just said, "Why, Lord, am I doing this every Sunday, particularly this Sunday? I am tired." To be honest with you, my attitude just plain stunk. When I got to Blacksburg, I had directions, but I couldn't find the way to get there, and nobody that I asked knew where Nazareth Baptist Church was located. I was running late, and didn't know if I was going to get there on time. Finally, I got the right directions. When I arrived, I realized why it was so hard to find. Nazareth Baptist Church was behind the woods on a dead-end road. God had to put that church there because no one else would have.

I pulled into the parking lot and still had the worst attitude. The preacher was on the front steps. It was 11:00 am, and I'm sure he was wondering what he was going to do if I didn't show. He probably had one leftover sermon that he could preach. He was out there pacing and looking for me. After pulling in, I asked myself, "What in the world is wrong with me?" I remembered this verse; "Amaziah did what was right in the eyes of the Lord, but not with a loyal heart." I said, "I'm doing what is right, but my heart is not in it." I got out of the car and on my knees and said "Lord, please forgive me." I asked for forgiveness for a number of things, but particularly my attitude. The pastor was on the front steps and he was all but saying, "Come on! Come on! We pray inside. We don't have time for you to pray out here. The service is beginning." So, I shut the door and ran into the church with him. I sat down and noticed my son and some of his buddies that played basketball with him at his school.

When I sat down in the front and got ready to preach, I realized that I didn't have my Bible. I asked the pastor if I could borrow his Bible. Well, can you imagine any pastor inviting someone and the guy not having his Bible? I was already late; I was praying out in the parking lot, and I didn't have my Bible. I guess it was evident that North Greenville was in real trouble if this was the president. I got up and didn't have my message and said, "Lord it has to be about you, it's not about me, anyway. You just show-out through me."

He gave me the message and to this day, I'm not sure what God said, but when we had the time of commitment, Tim's heart got touched by God. He was Bert's friend who was seven feet tall and stood head and shoulders above anybody in that church. He came running down that isle, grabbed hold of me, and just covered me up. He said, "I want Jesus in my heart. I accept Him. I believe He died on the cross for me. I believe it's a gift, through God's grace. I can now have everlasting life. I know right now that if I die, I will go to heaven." Oh, it was a rejoicing time.

I want you to realize how God works. I mentioned that I was at Nazareth Baptist Church in Blacksburg, South Carolina. It's behind the woods on a dead-end road. You can't find it. God had to put it there. Tim is from Australia. Only God could get a seven foot Australian in a country church in the middle of nowhere. It wasn't an accident. It was God's purpose. Let me also tell you, that if I had gone into that church, tried to preach, do what was right, and my heart not be in it, God could have still probably done it, but I would have missed a tremendous blessing. It would not have been successful, as well as not represented God well. I doubt very seriously that God would have been able to use that message through me, because his vessel had a sorry attitude.

If one has a genuine relationship with God, then you have changed and want to make a difference by being a servant of all. The team must be made up of servants, which leads to successful teamwork.

In most cases, almost every person, when asked about the tragedy of September 11, the towers in New York City, could say where they were when they heard about 9/11. I remember that it was on a Tuesday, and every Tuesday morning at North Greenville, I had my executive council meeting if I was in town, which meant all the vice presidents would come to a meeting with me. We had devotions at 8:45 am, and then we met and discussed what needed to be done at North Greenville. As a team, we work together on plans to help North Greenville be a better university. We had just started the meeting after the devotions when one of the ladies in the office came in and said, "You won't believe what just happened." She told us about it and we immediately stopped and prayed for the situation. Then we decided that we would go ahead and keep our classes going. Tell the professors in their prayer time with the classes to give more emphasis on the folks involved in 9/11. Then, maybe later that afternoon, we would have time to come together as a North Greenville family, after the class schedule is almost complete, and lift everyone up in a worship service. We went on and finished the meeting and I got back in the office.

All of a sudden, four or five students came bounding into my office without knocking. They said, "Dr. Epting, do you not know what's going on? Don't you know that there are terrorists attacking our nation? Aren't you aware of what's happening? You're our leader and nothing's going on. They are calling off classes at Notre Dame and Harvard and Stanford, and all kinds of other schools, universities, and colleges. They are praying and lifting this whole situation up and we're not doing anything. What's going on? You're our leader. You've got to make some decisions. We've got to do some of this."

I said, "Okay, okay, just sit down here and calm down. First of all, let me tell you that I will fail you. You don't need to be looking to me today. We need to look to God. He will never fail you. Second, I am glad these folks are stopping to pray and lifting this matter up, because as far as I know, the institutions that you have mentioned haven't done much of that in the past. Plus, at North Greenville, we don't have to stop to pray. We already pray in all of our classes and in everything we do. We start with prayer and devotion. The faculty will carry on just like usual. In addition, we are having a special service this afternoon." Thank goodness we don't have to change.

During this time, they were praying on the steps of the Capitol in Washington, DC, and they were talking about prayer. All the leaders were lifting it all up to God. We were becoming a very spiritual nation, all of a sudden.

The very next Sunday, when I went to preach, the parking lot was full and the service was full. I looked to the pastor and I asked, "Pastor, what's going on? Did they hear that I was coming to preach?" We both laughed because we knew that wasn't it. We knew that people were turning to God because of this tragedy… and the next Sunday and the next Sunday. They were talking about it in their families and the school systems. But the sad thing was, it wasn't long before things were back to normal again and we were treating God like a spare tire.

We only turn to Him when we need Him. We know He's there. We know He will be there for us. He loves us regardless. So many times, it's on an "as needed" basis. Back to normal, unfortunately, was no God in Washington, the families, or the school system. In this world today, we are turning from Him and we're not allowing Him to be number one in our lives. As far as I am concerned, there is no team or teamwork without a strong emphasis on God at all times.

The following puts 9/11 in proper prospective:

You say you will never forget where you were when you heard the news on September 11, 2001.

Neither will I.

I was on the 110th floor in a smoke-filled room with a man who called his wife to say "Good Bye." I held his fingers steady as he dialed. I gave him the peace to say, "Honey, I am not going to make it, but it is OK. I am ready to go."

I was with his wife when he called as she fed breakfast to their children. I held her up as she tried to understand his words and as she realized he wasn't coming home that night.

I was in the stairwell of the 23rd floor when a woman cried out to Me for help. "I have been knocking on the door of your heart for 50 years!" I said. "Of course, I will show you the way home – only
Believe in Me now."

I was at the base of the building with the priest ministering to the injured and devastated souls. I took him home to tend to his flock in Heaven. He heard my voice and answered.

I was on all four of those planes, in every seat, with every prayer. I was with the crew as they were overtaken. I was in the very hearts of the believers there, comforting and assuring them that their faith had saved them.

I was in Texas, Virginia, California, Michigan, Afghanistan. I was standing next to you when you heard the terrible news.

Did you sense Me?

I want you to know that I saw every face. I knew every name – though not all knew Me. Some met Me for the first time on the 86th floor.

Some sought Me with their last breath.

Some couldn't hear Me calling to them through the smoke and flames; "Come to Me…this way…take my hand." Some chose, for the final time, to ignore Me.

But I was there.

I did not place you in the tower that day. You may not know why, but I do. However, if you were there in that explosive moment in time, would you have reached for Me?

September 11, 2001, was not the end of the journey for you. But someday your journey will end. And I will be there for you as well. Seek Me now while I may be found. Then,

at any moment, you know you are
ready to go."

I will be in the stairwell of your final moments.

GOD

Authored by Stacey Randall

A real man/woman has a passion for God and is willing to lay down his/her life for Him. This is the kind of person who is needed on the team for strong teamwork and effective change. Teamwork that facilitates change is what allows Jesus Christ to make the difference in the hearts of others. And Jesus said, **"I know you can't, but I can!!!"**

Chapter 7
THE TOUCH OF THE MASTER'S HAND

There was a time when there was no refrigeration like we know it today. Everything had to be kept on ice. Well, it was late on a Saturday and the country store owner had worked long hours all week. Sunday was his day off, so he was ready to close up and go home. At about closing time, the little old lady in the community came to the door and said, "I know that you are about to close but I need a chicken for Sunday dinner. Please let me come into the store and buy a chicken." He begrudgingly said, "Come on in, but let's hurry."

They went to the icebox and the storeowner put his arm into the box and he pulled up a chicken. "Okay, here's your chicken. Pay me so we can go home." The old lady looked at the man and at the chicken and said, "That chicken looks a bit small. Can you get me another one?" So disgustingly, the storeowner put his arm in the icebox and moved his arm around, and realized that it was the only chicken in the box. Then the light came on. He said to himself, "I'm a salesman. If I am going to sell this one chicken that I have left, I've got to be more excited about trying to sell it."

So, he moved his arm around as if he had a whole bunch of chickens in the box when he had only that one. Then he pulled up that same chicken and he said, enthusiastically, "Here's another chicken. Look how big it is. I know you want this chicken. It's a great looking chicken." Well, the old lady looked at the man and looked at the chicken and said, "It does look bigger; but I guess what I'll have to do is take both of them chickens." The storeowner was being deceptive, or at least he was hedging on the truth, and he got caught.

There was no deception on my part. I knew that God had called me for such a time as this to be His leader at North Greenville. I knew that I needed to be a servant leader, and it had to be about the heart. I was driven by my love for God and people, and I like to think that I had a professional will and humility. My passion for the new mission was an important leadership attribute that helped inspire others to accept my vision. **I believe God had touched my leadership traits, which included: a sense of calling, desire for devoted service to God, the ability to cast a shared vision, service to fellow workers, and genuine love for others.** I tried to create a welcoming and friendly environment for an unending expression of love and concern for our students, which is better known as **"The Hug."** I sincerely believe that reaching out and loving them with no qualifiers served to promote student enrollment.

Additionally, I tried to be honest, competent, forward-looking, and inspiring, which hopefully gave quality to my relationships with our employees. In creating the vision, I continued to be vigilant in seeking input from others and establishing trust. This helped me build a sense of shared ownership and support for proposed changes. Most importantly, I tried to model the way. I chose to put the needs, aspirations, and interests of my fellow workers above my own through modeling a Christ-like example. If I have been successful with any of the above, it is because of **The Touch of the Master's Hand. The key to it all is for each one of us to be touched, so we can better allow God to touch others.**

In the days when an ice cream sundae cost much less, a ten-year-old entered a hotel coffee shop and sat down at a table. A waitress put a glass of water in front of him. "How much is an ice cream sundae?" he asked. "Fifty cents," replied the waitress. The little boy pulled his hand out of his pocket and studied the coins in it. "Well, how much is a plain dish of ice cream?" he inquired. By now, more people were waiting for a table and the waitress was growing impatient. "Thirty-five cents," she roughly replied. The little boy again counted his coins. "I'll have the plain ice cream," he said.

The waitress brought the ice cream, threw the bill on the table, and walked away. The little boy finished the ice cream, paid the cashier, and left. When the waitress came back, she began to cry as she wiped down the table. There, placed neatly beside the empty dish, were two nickels and five pennies. You see, he couldn't have the sundae because he had to have enough left to leave her a tip. I believe the little boy had been touched, in order to touch the waitress.

During my second month of college, our professor gave us a pop quiz. I was a conscientious student and breezed through the questions until I read the last one. "What is the first name of the woman who cleans the school?" Surely, this was some kind of joke. I had seen the cleaning woman several times. She was tall, dark-haired, and in her 50s. But, how would I know her name? I handed in my paper leaving the last question blank. Just before class ended, one student asked if that last question would count toward our quiz grade. "Absolutely!" said the professor. "In your careers, you will meet many people. All are significant. They deserve your attention and care even if all you do is smile and say, "Hello." Again, we are talking about being touched and touching others. I've never forgotten that lesson. I also learned her name was Judy.

Wishing to encourage her young son's progress on the piano, a mother took the boy to a Paderewski concert. After they were seated, the mother spotted an old friend in the audience and walked down the aisle to greet her. Seizing the opportunity to explore the wonders of the concert hall, the little boy rose and eventually explored his way through a door marked "NO ADMITTANCE."

When the house lights dimmed and the concert was about to begin, the mother returned to her seat and discovered the child was missing. Suddenly, the curtains parted and spotlights focused on the impressive Steinway on stage. In horror, the mother saw her little boy sitting at the keyboard, innocently picking out "Twinkle, Twinkle Little Star."

At that moment, the great piano master made his entrance, quickly moved to the piano and whispered in the boy's ear, "Don't quit. Keep playing." Then leaning over, Paderewski reached down with his left hand and begin filling in a bass part. Soon his right arm reached around to the other side of the child, and he added a running obbligato. Together, the old master and the young novice transformed what could have been a frightening situation into a wonderfully creative experience. The audience was so mesmerized that they couldn't recall what else the great master played... only the classic, "Twinkle, Twinkle Little Star."

Perhaps that is the way it is with God. What we can accomplish on our own is hardly noteworthy. We try our best, but the results aren't always gracefully flowing music. However, with the touch of the Master, our life's work can truly be beautiful. Next time you set out to accomplish great feats, listen carefully. You may hear the voice of the Master, whispering in your ear, "Don't quit. Keep playing!" May you feel His arms around you, and know that His hands are there helping you turn your feeble attempts into true masterpieces. **Life is more accurately measured by the lives you touch than by the things you acquire.** We should all touch someone today.

In Mark 1: 40-45, it starts out talking about a leper. Verse 40 says, "Now a leper came to Him, imploring Him, kneeling down to Him and saying to Him, 'If you are willing, You can make me clean.'" The interesting thing about that verse is the leper felt unclean, but he knew Jesus could cleanse him and he came to him on his knees. After all, shouldn't we come to the King on our knees? Looking at leprosy even today, when it goes untreated, it can be a horrible, horrible sight. It collapses the nose; it leads to ulcers; it destroys the sight; it causes infections, loss of fingers and toes. Untreated lepers are some of the worst-looking people you can imagine.

When my wife and I went to India, we knew they had at least four and a half million lepers in that country. When I went to be with these people, they wouldn't let me see them. Finally, in the back of the compound where I was serving, there was a tent of people with leprosy. I wanted to love on them, care for them, and let them know that Jesus loves them regardless. The man with leprosy said to Jesus, "If You are willing, You can make me clean." In verse 41, it said, "Then Jesus, moved with compassion, stretched out His hand and touched him, and said to him, 'I am willing: be cleansed.'" So many times, it just takes a Touch of the Master's hand.

Well, it was battered and scarred and the auctioneer felt it was hardly worth his while, to waste much time on the old violin, but he held it up with a smile. "Well, it sure ain't much but it's all we got left. I guess we ought to sell it, too. Now who's got a bid on this old violin? Just one more and we'll be through." And then he cried, "One, give me one dollar. Who'll make it two? Only two dollars? Who'll make it three? Three dollars twice, now that's a good price, now who's got a bid for me? Raise up your hand, don't wait any longer, the auction's about to end. Who's got four? Just one dollar more, to bid on this old violin."

Well, the air was hot and the people stood around as the sun was settin' low. From the back of the crowd, a gray-haired man came forward and picked up the bow. He wiped the dust from the old violin then he tightened up the strings. And then he played out a melody pure and sweet, sweeter than the angels sing. And when the music stopped, the auctioneer, with a voice that was quiet and low, he said, "Now who's got a bid for this old violin?" Then he held it up with the bow. And then he cried out, "One, give me one thousand? Who'll make it two? Only two thousand? Who'll make it three? Three thousand twice, you know that's a good price, come on, who's got a bid for me?" And the people cried out "What made the change? We don't understand." The auctioneer stopped and he said with a smile, "It was the touch of the master's hand."

You know there's many a man with his life out of tune, battered and scarred with sin. And he's auctioned cheap to a thankless world, much like that old violin. Oh, but then the Master comes, and the foolish crowd, they never understand, the worth of a soul, a change that is wrought by the touch of the Master's hand. Then he cried out, "One, give me one thousand? Who'll make it two? Only two thousand? Who'll make it three? Three thousand twice, now know that's a good price, but who's got a bid for me?" And the people cried out, "What made the change? We

don't understand." The auctioneer stopped and he said
with a smile, "It was the touch of the master's hand."

– by Myra 'Brooks' Welch.

"As soon as He had spoken, immediately the leprosy left him and he was cleansed." He was not only cleansed on the outside. He was cleansed from the inside out. Verse 43 says, "And He strictly warned him and sent him away at once," Verse 44, "and said to him, 'See that you say nothing to anyone; but go your way, show yourself to the priest, and offer for your cleansing those things which Moses commanded, as a testimony to them.'" Verse 45, "However, he went out and began to proclaim it freely, and to spread the matter, so that Jesus could no longer openly enter the city, but was outside in deserted places; and they came to Him from every direction."

What was Jesus really doing? Give the man with leprosy a break. There was no way that he wasn't going to tell everybody. When we get Jesus and He cleanses us inside and out, we need to be excited about it. We want to tell the whole world. I know what it is, here's the secret to evangelism. Have you ever heard someone say to another, "I have a secret and I am going to tell only you? Please be sure you tell no one else." The next thing you know, that person that was told the secret inevitably goes to another person and says, "Now don't you tell anybody that I've been given this secret and I'm going to tell only you." Before you know it, it spreads like wildfire. There's the secret.

"Next Sunday, we're going to have real revival and we're going to share Jesus. It's going to be a wonderful time of worship and lifting Jesus up, but don't tell anybody. Keep it a secret!" And then hopefully, it would be so crowded and so many people would show up that we would have to go out to deserted places. Maybe I'm being somewhat facetious. The point is: If you have really been cleansed, why wouldn't you want to let the whole world know about it? Why wouldn't you want to share Jesus?

A young man was getting ready to graduate from college.
For many months he had admired a beautiful sports car
in a dealer's showroom, and knowing his father could well

afford it, he told him that was all he wanted. As Graduation Day approached, the young man awaited signs that his father had purchased the car. Finally, on the morning of his graduation, his father called him into his private study. His father told him how proud he was to have such a fine son, and told him how much he loved him. He handed his son a beautifully wrapped gift box. Curious, but somewhat disappointed, the young man opened the box and found a lovely, leather-bound Bible, with the young man's name embossed in gold. Angrily, he raised his voice to his father and said, "With all your money you give me a Bible?" He then stormed out of the house, leaving the Bible.

Many years passed and the young man was very successful in business. He had a beautiful home and wonderful family, but realizing his father was very old, he thought perhaps he should go to him. The young man had not seen his father since that graduation day. But before he could make arrangements, he received a telegram telling him his father had passed away, and willed all his possessions to his son. He needed to come home immediately and take care of things. When the son arrived at his father's house, sudden sadness and regret filled his heart. He began to search through his father's important papers and found the still-new Bible, just as he'd left it years ago. With tears, he opened the Bible and began to turn the pages. His father had carefully underlined a verse, Matthew 7:11, "If you then, being evil, know how to give good gifts to your children, how much more will your Father who is in heaven give good things to those who ask Him!" As he read those words, a car key dropped from the back of the Bible. It had a tag with a dealer's name; the same dealer who had the sports car he had desired many years ago. On the tag was the date of his graduation, and the words **PAID IN FULL.**

How many times do we miss God's blessings because they are not packaged as we expected?

In Romans 10: 9-10 it says, "That if you confess with your mouth the Lord Jesus and believe in your heart that God has raised Him from the dead, you will be saved. For with the heart one believes unto righteousness, and with the mouth confession is made unto salvation." North Greenville University, as well as Jimmy Epting, needed to be touched, because if we're touched, we have a better chance, a better opportunity, to touch others.

> After a few of the usual Sunday evening hymns, the church's pastor slowly stood up, walked over to the pulpit and, before he gave his sermon for the evening, briefly introduced a guest minister who was in the service. In the introduction, the pastor told the congregation that the guest minister was one of his dearest childhood friends, and that he wanted him to have a few moments to greet the church and share whatever he felt would be appropriate for the service.

> With that, an elderly man stepped up to the pulpit and began to speak. "A father, his son, and a friend of his son were sailing off the Pacific coast," he began, "when a fast-approaching storm blocked any attempt to get back to shore. The waves were so high, that even though the father was an experienced sailor, he could not keep the boat upright; the three were swept into the ocean as the boat capsized." The old man hesitated for a moment, making eye contact with two teenagers who were, for the first time since the service began, looking somewhat interested in his story.

> The aged minister continued, "Grabbing a rescue line, the father had to make the most excruciating decision of his life: to which boy he would throw the other end of the lifeline. He only had seconds to make the decision. The father knew that his son was a Christian and he also knew that his son's friend was not. The agony of his decision cannot be matched by the torrent of the waves. As the father yelled out, 'I love you son!' he threw out the lifeline to his son's friend. By the time the father had pulled the

*friend back to the capsized boat, his son had disappeared
beneath the raging swell into the black of night. His body
was never recovered.*

*By this time the two teenagers were sitting up straight in
the pews, anxiously waiting for the next words to come
out of the old minister's mouth. "The father," he continued,
"knew his son would step into eternity with Jesus, and he
could not bear the thought of his son's friend stepping into
eternity without Jesus. Therefore, he sacrificed his son to
save the son's friend. How great is the love of God that He
should do the same for us! Our heavenly Father sacrificed
His only begotten Son that we could be saved. I urge you
to accept His offer to rescue you and take hold of the
lifeline He is throwing out to you in this service."*

*With that, the old man turned and sat back down in his
chair as silence filled the room. The pastor again walked
slowly to the pulpit and delivered a brief sermon with an
invitation at the end. However, no one responded to the
appeal.*

*Within minutes after the service ended, the two teenagers
were at the old man's side. "That was a nice story," politely
stated one of the boys, "but I don't think it was very realistic for the father to give up his only son's life in hopes that
the other boy would become a Christian." "Well, you've
got a point there," the old man replied, glancing down at
his worn Bible. A big smile broadened his narrow face; he
once again looked up at the boys and said, "It sure isn't
very realistic, is it? But I'm standing here today to tell you
that story gives me a glimpse, just a glimpse, of what it
must've been like for God to give up His son for me. You
see… I was that father and your pastor is my son's friend."*

God does want you to be touched, so that you can touch others.
That's what has happened at North Greenville.

And Jesus said, **"I know you can't, but I can!!!"**

Chapter 8
INFLUENCE ON ANOTHER
THROUGH GIVING

We like to relate the story that a number of people died in the upper Greenville County area. Some from Greenville, some from Travelers Rest, some from Greer and other places in the area that are not far from Tigerville, South Carolina. They all arrived in Heaven at the same time. Of course, the one who met them at the pearly gates was good ole' Peter and he couldn't wait to show them around the area. He showed them the crystal-clear waters and the streets of gold, all the mansions, and they were just having a big time looking around. The next thing you knew, they were in a horrible section of Heaven. It looked like a dungeon. It was dark and the people were moaning and groaning. They had chains attached to them. They couldn't move out of that area and all the people from Greer, Greenville, Travelers Rest, and the other places were upset. They said, "What is all of this? This is Heaven. We thought this was a beautiful, wonderful place." Peter said, "Now listen folks, don't you worry one bit about those people. All those folks are from Tigerville, South Carolina, where North Greenville University is located, and they just keep wanting to go home on the weekends."

The bottom line is, North Greenville and Tigerville are God's country. It's the next best thing to Heaven. North Greenville is in a great location. We're far enough from the city that we can be out and enjoy the beautiful countryside and mountains, at the foothills of the Blue Ridge Mountains. At the same time, it is just a short trip to get into some of the city life. You've got the best of both worlds. I always say that, "North Greenville University and Tigerville, South Carolina, are the next best things to heaven, and we want to welcome you to God's country."

> *A student used to tell this story on me. There was a man by the name of Jack Daniels. Now Jack was an older man who had made a little bit of money in the stock market, so he retired at an early age from an architecture company where he used to design buildings.*

> *Jack had always wanted to travel abroad to see the various types of architecture. Now Jack was not a religious man; but he loved the design of churches and cathedrals.*

> *Jack decided that on his first trip he would go halfway around the world to China. While he was in Beijing, he went into one of the famous cathedrals there. He took many pictures and was very amazed. On his way out, he saw a red telephone near the "Holy Water" with a sign in English and Chinese that said $1 million a call. Jack was very confused, so he asked the priest what the phone was for, and why it was $1 million. The priest told him it was a direct line to God. Jack blew it off and went about his way.*

> *Later that month Jack was in Europe. He went into another church there and went through his same routine of taking pictures. Again, on his way out he saw a red phone with the same sign, $1 million a call. Again, Jack blew it off.*

> *This kind of thing went on for a year. Jack would go into a church or cathedral and would always see that red phone with a price of $1 million a call.*

> *One day Jack's nephew told him about his university in Tigerville, South Carolina, and how they had just renovated the chapel.*

> *Jack went to North Greenville University and was so amazed by the chapel and all the new renovations done*

to it. On his way out he saw that same red phone, but this time the sign said 35 cents per call. Jack was very confused and proceeded to ask Jimmy Epting what the phone was for and why it was only 35 cents, because it had been $1 million everywhere else.

Jimmy simply said it is a direct line to God and it was only 35 cents because it was a local call.

Although the location plays a significant role in providing an excellent environment for influencing others, the right kind of influence starts with the individual and his/her attitude toward and about others. As students came to North Greenville, and as faculty/staff became a part of it, we all wanted to be the right kind of influence on each other, and especially be the right kind of influence on the students. So the first question is, "What kind of influence are you on another?" "Do you know that you influence, directly or indirectly, over 3,000 people in your lifetime?"

In 1990, the year before I became president of North Greenville, I entered into the restaurant business with a friend. My wife was pretty much against it and didn't want to do it at that time. My friend had a lot of experience in the restaurant business and I was just going to put up the funds to make it happen. I would not have to do anything else, and the profit and loss sheet showed that we would easily profit through this business. Well, it wasn't long before my partner, my friend, came to me about the restaurant business not doing well. We called it "The Fishnet," and it was a seafood restaurant. The biggest problem was that he hadn't been able to pay the taxes. My wife and I, particularly my wife, had to get more involved in the business. It was located on the other side of Greenville, roughly 45 minutes to an hour away from Tigerville.

The restaurant business was going down the tubes and I was losing all the money we had in our savings. I had just become president of North Greenville and the restaurant business was a total loss, barely surviving, if at all. North Greenville was a total loss, barely surviving, if at all. I had two places that I was trying to save. At this time, I thought maybe if we open up another restaurant in Travelers Rest, another Fishnet, "Fishnet II," we could make some money. Well, you don't start another restaurant when the other one is dying. The real purpose for starting another restaurant was to eliminate the partnership with my friend.

Gretchen and I, (Gretchen reluctantly), opened the second restaurant in Travelers Rest, S.C. We gave the other restaurant to my partner, as well as took all the bills and all the debt. We tried to start all over again with the Fishnet Restaurant in Travelers Rest, which was only about 15 minutes from where we lived in Tigerville. It was a slow go at that point and we had no money. All our money was gone. Our only income was what I was being paid to work at North Greenville, and I took a pay cut to come as president because they could not afford to pay me a reasonable salary. We had very little. Basically, everything we did have, we had lost; what was left was banked on the second restaurant surviving. At the time, we had the restaurant open Tuesday through Sunday.

Sunday lunch was a very good day for us. The church people would come, but we all realized unfortunately, especially our waitresses, that church people can be awfully hard on servers. They mistreated our folks. You wouldn't have realized they had been to church that day. There may be a table of ten and they would leave a dollar for our waitresses. That's sad to say, but true. My whole family was working there and I was out preaching on Sundays, so I couldn't be there. I was trying to represent North Greenville, but every Friday and Saturday night, if I wasn't doing something for North Greenville, I would be in the restaurant cooking and trying to do my part. Gretchen was running the restaurant, trying to do her part, and all three of my children – Daphne, Bert, and Paul – were working in there as hard as possible. We were really trying to make a go of it.

I remember on a Saturday night I had to stay and was cleaning the fryers, getting everything ready for the next day. I had to go preach three or four hours away the next morning. Later I rode home with tears just flowing down my face. I said, "Lord, what have I gotten myself into? I have two lost causes here and I'm just sinking, going under." And He said two things to me very clearly. Number one was, "You need to close on Sunday," and number two, "You need to learn everything about cooking and working in the kitchen, so you can do a better job of preparing food for the restaurant." At about the same time, the Lord told Gretchen to close the restaurant on Sunday as well. The next Sunday was the last Sunday we were open. That was the best and most profitable day of the week for us; but we closed it up, knowing our family needed to be in church. As soon as we closed up on Sunday, God replaced it completely with money from the week. We never missed it.

After about a week of writing all the menus down, following them, and doing a lot of the cooking, our best cook came to me and said, "I'm going to have to give you a two-week notice. I can't cook anymore." I had already started to learn, but the next two weeks I spent even more time learning everything he knew about cooking, so I could train others and do my part as well. God had told me what I needed to do.

The business started doing better, even doing well. North Greenville started doing better, and doing well. I had turned it over to God, and what was really neat, I became a good cook for the Friday and Saturday nights. God used that restaurant to help North Greenville not only survive, but stabilize. All the people in Travelers Rest and the surrounding areas would come to "The Fishnet" to eat, and they would see the president walking out covered in flour from head to toe and somewhat dirty from the cooking. And they would see the president's wife and children slaving away out front, serving people and cleaning tables. I am convinced the people in the area said, "You know, those people aren't all bad. There must be something good about them. They are trying to lead North Greenville and they are doing this kind of work. Maybe we ought to support, not only the restaurant, but also North Greenville more." God used it in a very special way and people knew we were Christians by the way we handled things. We tried to be the right kind of influence and have a Christ-like influence on everyone we came in contact with, especially in the restaurant.

It wasn't long before we had all our money back that we had lost. We were even financially stable again, and three different people came in wanting to buy the business. We ended up selling it for a profit, and gladly. We would probably have sold it just to break even and be out of it, because North Greenville kept needing more and more of my time, my wife's time, and our family's time. I would like to think the restaurant business was a good influence on others.

Another great example of an influence on me dealt with two individuals and my cars. The first individual was Jim Anthony. Jim Anthony, in 1991 when I started at North Greenville, started "The Cliffs at Glassy," the first of many of his developments. I had met him once at an auction, but had just said hello to him. I called and said, "I need to come up. We're neighbors and I need to meet you and get to know you better." So, he allowed me to come see him. I had a car, an old Buick that belonged to the last three presidents, which was on its very last leg. I don't think it was going to make it another day. I was driving up to the top of Glassy Mountain, which is just a few miles from North Greenville University – the closest mountain to Tigerville. It has a winding, gravel road and it was a chore to get to the top in that car. It started smoking on the way up to the little sales cabin behind a gravel parking lot on the top of the mountain. I pulled into that gravel parking lot and there was a man sitting on the front porch of the sales house. I tried to turn off the car, but it wouldn't turn off. Finally, I put the key into the off position with the engine still trying to run. I slammed the door and it finally stopped.

As I walked up on the steps, I thought the man was Jim Anthony, but I wasn't sure. Then, I realized it was indeed Jim sitting on the porch. I went over to him and introduced myself to him again. I said, "I'm Jimmy Epting, president at North Greenville. I appreciate you seeing me." He said, "One thing for sure, you need a new car." The Lord put it in my mind at that point to say, "Well, Mr. Anthony, that's why I'm here today. I need for you to give me a new car." In two or three weeks, he called me up and told me to go over to George Coleman Ford in Travelers Rest, S.C. There would be three or four cars waiting, and I was to select one. He would give it to the University for me to use. What an influence!

After a few years, because of my heavy traveling, this car began breaking down on a regular basis. I remember being pulled by a wrecker onto the front campus and I was in the front seat with the wrecker driver with the car being pulled behind. Some faculty members saw me and my car being pulled. You could tell they thought it was quite humorous because of their laughter. I was still out working as hard as I could go and had probably just run that car into the ground. I needed another car. I didn't know the owner of the Toyota, Lexus, Porsche, Volvo, and Jaguar car dealerships, but a friend told me about a man named Terry Wall. Terry Wall owned all those dealerships. I called Mr. Wall and asked about seeing him. I went to see him and told him I needed a new car. He saw the one I had and he said, "Yes, you do."

It wasn't long before he had me come over and said, "Go out there and pick out any car you want. It's yours." I test drove a Lexus. I test drove a Toyota. I test drove a Volvo and different cars. I had to be careful because, you see, as a university president, I'm just an old beggar. As a matter of a fact, if you read this, you need to be sure to remind my wife to put on my tombstone, "It came to pass, the beggar died." A beggar can't have too nice a car, but you still want to have a nice car.

I was trying all the cars with one of the salesmen and I was like a kid in a candy factory. When I was driving a Toyota Avalon, at the time they were just becoming available, the salesman was in the backseat and he said, "Man, why are you driving this car? You can have any car out here. Let's go get that nice Lexus over there." All of a sudden, the Lord just put me on a guilt trip and I said, "You know, this isn't right. I am going to take this car. I should be thankful for this nice car. Anyway, I can't have too nice of a car. This is the one I'm taking." Can you imagine someone saying pick out any car you want? What an influence! Both of these men have been very supportive with scholarships and in so many other ways.

When Mr. Wall sold his businesses, Dave Edwards of Dave Edwards Toyota in Spartanburg, SC, provided a Toyota Avalon for me to use as I served the Lord. When I went to ask him about providing the car, he did not hesitate and was so willing to give to God's ministry. Rodney Back, his General Manager, helped make it happen and he and his wife, Chris, supported us financially.

Many car dealers helped the university over the years by giving vehicles to own or use. Kevin Whitaker, Dick Smith, George and Greg

Coleman were four of them. Also, Billy Jackson of Dick Brooks Honda provided vehicles and financial support for facilities.

A dear lady, Josephine Roof, in 1991-92 went to her lawyer, Alvin Johnson, who had attended North Greenville and went on to Wofford College, as well as USC. He helped her get a lot of the funding that she needed when she got her divorce. She was in his office one day and said, "You know I want to leave my money to somewhere special. She saw his diplomas on the wall. He had three and she said, "Which one of those schools would you recommend that I leave my money?" He said without hesitation that it was North Greenville, because "North Greenville gave me my start." It was a two-year school at the time, and if he hadn't gotten those two years, he wouldn't have gone on to another school and become a lawyer. So, Josephine Roof never put foot on our campus, but left us a wonderful, huge gift for our endowment. That was such a good shot in the arm to the university (at that time, still a college). You never know about the influence you may have on another.

And then there were others along the way that have done so much. I hate to mention some of them and not others because of the possibility of not recognizing someone special. All of them have been an influence on North Greenville and me.

Next, I have to mention Joe and Eleanor Hayes. They provided scholarships and buildings, and so much more, especially when I first arrived as president and over the first five years or so. They gave property and other gifts to make things happen. They have just always been there for North Greenville and me. Joe served on the Board with every president from Donnan to Epting. On January 16, 2019, Dr. Joe F. Hayes, Sr. went to be with our Lord, and I was told that his last words on this earth were to me: "Jimmy, I love you!"

Then, there is Arnold and Pauline Emery. They have done the same by giving property and other gifts for scholarships, facilities, and programs. They were always committed to serving the Lord at North Greenville. Arnold was Chairman of the Board over the years at least eight times. He attended the North Greenville Academy and got his Associate, four-year, and Honorary Doctorate degrees from North Greenville over the years. They have always lived close to the school and given their all to it! This couple were such strong supporters.

Lee and Barbara McCormick went to North Greenville and love the school. Like so many couples, they met here and eventually married. They have given a lot to help the university through the years, and they have done their very best not to get any credit for it, but to give all the credit to the Lord. Lee and Barbara not only made gifts. They gave their time and efforts. They were tremendous servants who God used in a great way at the school. What an influence!

One real special couple was Neb and Martha Cline. When Neb was alive, they did a lot for scholarships and buildings. When Neb died, Martha became like my second mother. Oh, how I loved her. Both of them are in Heaven today. I had the opportunity to see her at least two or three times every week and to take her to Duke in Durham, N.C., to the doctor for a cancerous growth on her leg. We would make trips together. I was able to take her on a cruise. She made gifts to scholarship programs and to residence halls on campus.

She was determined and committed to our Fine Arts department, the Cline School of Music, and to the school becoming a Steinway University. We became one of 65 or 70 institutions of any kind, anywhere in the world, that is a Steinway University. This recognition meant that every piano played on the campus would be a Steinway piano. Mama Cline, two professors, Jackie Griffin and Fabio Parrini, and I went to New York to the Steinway Company. She couldn't walk very well, but that day she went over the whole building. We watched as she checked out how the Steinways were made, from the wood coming in from the yard outside to the final product. We went into the piano room, where all the pianos had been finished. Then, all the Steinways were played that would come to North Greenville because of her wonderful generosity.

Almost every Sunday that I was preaching, I would come back by and spend time with her. She was so smart and she knew so many things about the Greenville area and the people. She would keep me aware of what was going on in the news because I never had time to watch it myself. You talk about an influence: Mama Cline was as special as they come.

Then, there is Melvin and Dollie Younts. They were so very supportive of the University. North Greenville enjoys the Younts Football Stadium, the Younts Wellness Center, the Younts scholarships, and all kind of wonderful facilities on our campus because of Melvin and Dollie Younts. This also includes a significant commitment for the Arena/Worship Center. They were givers! In July, 2018, Dollie went to heaven and we will miss her.

Russell and Ruth Ashmore continued their financial support from my first day as president through the present time. Ruth, who has gone to Heaven, always made sure they gave to the different scholarship funds, and Russell, through his company, covered our asphalt and grading needs on campus. Because of their generosity, North Greenville enjoys The Ashmore Baseball Field.

All these folks have made a tremendous difference, along with Ralph and Marion Hendricks. North Greenville enjoys the Ralph and Marion Hendricks scholarship program for students out of Hillcrest and Woodmont high schools, along with the Ralph and Marion Hendricks Fieldhouse. Also, they provided the necessary funds for the President's Box in the future Arena/Worship Center. In February, 2019, Ralph went to be with the Lord at the age of 101. He was so special to me and I will miss him.

The giving spirit of Sam and Angie Kelly has been a tremendous influence on me. They have been so involved in giving of themselves and gifts. Gretchen and I remember so well the evening when they had dinner with us in our home and committed the gift for The Sam and Angie Kelly Strength and Conditioning Center (it must have been Gretchen's good cooking that made the difference).

Elton and Doris Todd continued to give all through the years. North Greenville has a couple of buildings with their names on them in addition to their scholarship program. Doris was a beautiful lady – inside and out. She is with the Lord and we miss her.

Then, there was Tom and Edna Hartness, who I got to know at another university. I fell in love with them and I think they fell in love with me. They liked what we were doing at North Greenville. While we could never replace the other university, they were always eager to help NGU as well. North Greenville has a Residence Hall and the President's Dining Hall with their names on them. They made wonderful gifts to North Greenville when they were alive. Also, Pat, their son, and his wife, Mary Lou, continued Pat's parents' spirit of giving with their support of facilities and scholarships.

Another couple who were supporters of another university was Jimmy and JoAnn Rogers. Although that school was their first love, they appreciated all we were trying to do at North Greenville University. Jimmy and I had a wonderful relationship and this fine couple provided various gifts. Also, they included North Greenville in a major way in their estate planning. Jimmy has gone on to be with Jesus. I sure miss him and his contagious laugh.

There was a sweet lady by the name of Georgia Roberson. Her husband's name was Marshall, and after his ministry days, he did well in business. Georgia wanted to recognize him and keep his memory going strong after his death. We met with her and she loved what we were doing at North Greenville. She gave a gift to pay for a Residence Hall and then she said she was going to be sure that she left North Greenville in her will when she died. She got sick and had some health problems. We didn't have any idea how much she would leave behind, but it turns out that when she died, she left the biggest gift ever bequeathed to North Greenville University. Half was for scholarships and half was to be used wherever it was needed. She was a dear lady and I enjoyed going to see her and spending time with her. She just loved to come to campus, when she could, and see the students.

Grover and Darla Todd wanted to honor her father, Vance Shreckengast, who was a great servant of God and is having a fantastic time in heaven, by providing the gift to build The Vance Tennis Complex. Because of them, the tennis teams and students can now have a first-class facility to play tennis. They are a wonderful couple and are definitely givers.

Gary and Betty Jo Glenn have been wonderful supporters of the athletic program with the gifts of cars and the new softball stadium to honor our long-time coach and Athletic Director, Jan McDonald. Their generosity and positive attitude were a breath of fresh air. They remain so special to North Greenville and me.

Dallah and Ann Forrest have been best friends and also strong supporters of NGU Fine Arts. Dallah attended North Greenville and later taught a few classes. They played a major role in raising and providing funds for the Fine Arts Center. Dallah has been and continues to be a tremendous influence on me because of his spirit of giving. He and Ann are a special couple.

Another special couple is Walt and Christine Brashier. They have done so much through the years and continue to support God's ministry at North Greenville through gifts for scholarships, programs, and buildings. They gave the major gift to start the Graduate School. In 2014, I went to see them because they had given another building in Greenville to house the Graduate School, and we decided to name this facility after one of their sons, Tim. He was a special person and went on to be with the Lord. I was going to show them what the sign would look like with Tim Brashier on it for that building.

Then, the Lord put on their hearts to help with what we called the Legacy Building, a new 5,000 seat Arena/Worship Center, which is to be built in the near future. I had gone over to have a "mater" sandwich with them and show them the picture of the signage. I told them that some of the folks at North Greenville wanted the Legacy Building to have Gretchen's and my name on it. I told everyone that I didn't want my name on anything. I wanted it to be about the Lord and not about me. Also, I wanted, if someone made a $3 million-dollar gift, them to have the naming rights. I told Walt and Christine about that on the front porch of their house as we were eating sandwiches. Walt looked over at Christine and first of all said, "You need to have your name on that building." I said, "I don't know about that." Then Walt and Christine looked at me and said, "You have been there for so many years and done so much, you need to have your name on it."

Walt looked over to Christine and said, "Why don't we just do $1 million dollars?" Christine didn't say anything at first, but then shoved two fingers into his face and he said, "Two million?" She said,

"Yes! We've got to have $1 million for Gretchen, as well." It got quiet and he looked over at her and said, "Why don't we just do the $3 million?" She said, "That would be fine with me." He looked over at me and said, "There is one stipulation: We have to have Gretchen's and your names on it. How do we make that happen?"

I gave him North Greenville's vice president's name and phone number, and he called him and got it worked out. Walt turned to me while he was on the phone with him and said, "He said he could make it happen," which I knew he would. When he hung up, I hollered and carried on and hugged and kissed on them. Christine said, "Dr. Epting, you can holler all you want out here. No one is going to hear you." The next thing she said was, "Dr. Epting, do you need an aspirin?" I guess I was getting so excited and carried away that she felt like my heart might need some help. What an influence! The absolute best way anyone could be an influence or be the best kind of influence is by being a giver.

I heard a story of someone calling a university office and telling the secretary that he wanted to speak to the head hog. The secretary said, "We don't have one." Then the man said, "I want to give $50,000 to the school, but I'll only deal with the head hog." The secretary then said, "I think I hear the little porker coming now." At North Greenville University, we were all aware that it takes a lot of giving for God to do His work. Giving of self and resources is vitally important.

A man came up to the pastor, and you couldn't help but notice that both ears had white gauze wrapped around them. The pastor was good friends with Frank, the man with the white gauze on his ears, and asked about it. He thought it might be plastic surgery or something. Frank said he didn't get to the cleaners this past week so he was ironing a shirt for church and the phone was right by the iron. When it rang, he picked up the iron instead of the phone. The pastor looked puzzled and asked what happened to the other ear. Frank said they called back again. When you are after folks to give, you have to keep calling and keep going back to them. You have to keep asking.

When it comes to giving, you should know that it is more blessed to give than to receive, and we must not cause God to get our attention a second time. Just like when Frank was called a second time. And, in addition, we must be sure that we do not take advantage of someone who tries or wants to give. Again, a cheerful giver can be the best influence on another.

A man and his wife, Mr. and Mrs. Clounts, were visiting the church and the pastor gave a plea, a very emotional plea, on the needs of the building fund. At the end of the service on the way out, they pulled the pastor over to the side and said they would give $5,000. The next Sunday as they were visiting the church, they noticed in the bulletin that it said, "Praise the Lord! Mr. and Mrs. Clounts, new attendees to our church, have pledged to give $50,000 to our new sanctuary. As you can imagine, they had trouble sitting through the sermon, and after the service they asked the pastor about it. They said, "It must be a mistake; we said $5,000."

The pastor apologized profusely, and after talking about it, the couple finally said, "If we could pay it over three years, we may be able to do it." The pastor was relieved and said since it was the lead gift, "We would like you to designate the verse that goes over the beam right in front of the church for all the people to see. They did. And on the day of the unveiling, with Mr. and Mrs. Clounts and the congregation all there, the veil was dropped and the verse was Matthew 25:35. "I was a stranger and you took me in."

Therefore, when it comes to giving, let's make sure God doesn't have to get our attention again, don't take advantage of anyone, and let's look squarely at ourselves.

I am reminded of the man and his wife who came down the aisle, and the woman asked, "Did you put anything in the offering plate?" He said, "No, but I prayed someone else would." Do you truly believe that it is more blessed to give than to receive? You see, the emphasis is on the giver, and his or her happiness. In understanding the meaning of giving, one must know God as "the giver of every good and perfect gift" – James 1:17. **Therefore, one's giving will follow a commitment to God as an act of religious worship that influences others.**

In Acts 20:32-36 it says, "And now, brethren, I commend you to God, and to the word of his grace, which is able to build you up, and to give you an inheritance among all them which are sanctified. I have coveted no man's silver, or gold, or apparel. Yes, you yourselves know, that these hands have provided for my necessities, and to those who were with me. I have shown you in every way, by laboring like this, that you must support the weak. And remember the words of the Lord Jesus, that He said, 'It is more blessed to give than to receive.' And when he had said these things, he knelt down and prayed with them all."

There are some very important messages in Act 20:32-36. First is a commitment to God. Second, do not covet. Third, we need to work hard. Fourth, we need to give. Fifth, we need to pray. These verses jumped out at me and helped me realize that people give because their commitment commands it. What a difference that takes place in giving and receiving. It is one thing to give what you can afford to give, but a totally different experience occurs when one gives sacrificially or what one cannot really afford to give, as with the widow in Luke 21. She gave all the living that she had. When one gives sacrificially, this giver becomes the best influence one could ever be on another.

A church was having the Christmas Eve service, which was the last service before the New Year in which they could receive funds to make their budget. At this service, there was a man and wife visiting, Mr. and Mrs. Bradshaw. The pastor stopped halfway through the service and said, "I have a real burden. We are short on making this year's budget. I want to pray about it and ask that, if you are led, come down and give to the Lord so we can meet our budget." Many came, among them a dear old lady walked up to the pastor and handed him something and said a few words.

After the lady sat down, the pastor could not go on. With tears in his eyes he told the congregation that this lady's husband had died a few months ago and all she had left to her name was this wedding band. She wanted to give to God for his work at the church and to meet the budget. It was perhaps worth $500, he said. Immediately, Mr. Bradshaw came forward and gave $5,000 for the ring, ten times its worth, and gave the ring back to the lady. Giving her all ended up multiplying the gift and influencing others to give, and give abundantly.

If there is one thing I have learned, it is not to compromise my faith when giving. You see, we are in the Good News business to bring mankind the eternal message of God's love in Jesus Christ. Therefore, we must remain focused on our primary course – pleasing God first. **Whatever God orders, He pays for it; and if He hasn't paid for it, maybe He didn't order it.** When we give, we should ask the fundamental question: Is this helping us accomplish the most important thing God has called us to? Billy Graham has been successful through all these years because he has only one mission and one message – Jesus Christ, Savior and Lord. It is never compromised to fulfill the primary purpose, which leads to never knowing the influence you may have on another.

As we focus on the primary course – the Good News business – we must not compromise and be a cheerful giver – remembering that our primary course must be pleasing to our primary source. Are you willing to commit all you have to Him, which will result in being the right kind of influence?

A man's brother gave him a new car and he took it to a rough neighborhood. As he parked it, a dirty little boy came up and said, "I will watch it for you. It is so pretty. Where did you get it?" "My brother gave it to me," he said. The little boy said, "I wish." Then the man interrupted and said, "I know, you wish your brother would give you a new car." "Oh no, I wish I could give my brother a car like that," said the little boy. What a wonderful attitude! What a good giving spirit!

As I try to remember others who have given to North Greenville, again, I hope I don't leave out any important folks. There was Henry Branyon, who went on to be with the Lord, but gave a wonderful gift for scholarships to help students who are studying in different programs. There was Jacks and Deborah Tingle. They have two buildings with the Tingle name on it and both Jacks and Deborah gave a lot of their lives to North Greenville. They were there through some tough times when the school was struggling.

When we were building the athletic facilities, Tony and Margaret Fogle donated truckloads of sod so we could have nice fields. Don Ward is such a special friend, as was his wife, Mary June, before her death. Don always, every year, helped students come to school and gave to the athletic program and other programs. He always gave sacrificially and more than was expected. Jim and Ann Black have been so special to North Greenville over the years. They have been faithful givers and ambassadors. Jerry and Martha Fowler – both of them are gone on to be with the Lord. They did a lot through the years for scholarships and facilities.

Another great couple was Eddie, who died a few years ago, and his wife, Kathy Runion. I will never forget when I went to see Eddie. He was one of the few that didn't turn his back on the university. When I went to him and told him that I needed his help, he immediately stepped up. When he went on to be with the Lord, Kathy helped provide the funding for one of the facilities on the NGU campus, in memory of Eddie. Zelda Rosti came forward, in memory of her husband, and provided funds for a building. Jack and Patti Billingsley gave to the Billingsley Theatre and helped to organize a fundraiser for the facility. Paul and Mildred Wood gave to help with the learning center and scholarships. There was James and Ruth Howard who gave property to help build a residence hall. There was Greg and Bobbie Horton, who gave to scholarships and also a residence hall.

Then, there was Nancy Hoy, who made a significant gift for the Craft/Hemphill Evangelism and Christian Worldview center. Her gift made such a tremendous difference, as did the gifts from Ira and Betty Jo Craft and Richard and Wilma Smith. Marvin and Noba Vaughn left a significant gift through their will for endowment, which provides many scholarships. Jimmy and Jean Cox gave their time and gifts to assist in many areas at the school. Jimmy was always willing to give his knowledge and efforts to assist with the planning of facilities. They are so special to North Greenville and me.

Also, we appreciate folks like Glenn and Joyce Bridges, who introduced some of these donors to the university. They not only made good gifts to the university to support in every way, but they encouraged others. Another special couple was Dan and Martha Boling. Their gifts over the years helped pay the costs of many students, and one of their major gifts made a tremendous difference in building the new Fine Arts Center. Mac Snyder, a special friend, always provided gifts for vehicles, scholarships, and facilities. Larry Stokes, who attended North Greenville, helped start the annual golf tournament fundraiser for athletics. He and Jacks Tingle, another alum, were responsible for over $1 million raised by organizing it and then, through support of it over the years.

Mike and Anne Burns were good financial supporters over the years. Mike played a major role in coordinating the building of the football facilities. Harry and Doris Mansfield loved another university but were willing to help North Greenville. They supported the golf tournament and the scholarship programs. Hewlett and Lucile Sullivan gave many gifts to scholarships and facilities. Hewlett was so very special to me and always gave me good advice. I sure did miss him when he went to be with the Lord. Lucile continues their support.

The Pepsi Company of Greenville, South Carolina, provided significant support through the years. John Gregory was the General Manager and got the school to be an all Pepsi/Mtn. Dew campus in the 80s. When Wayne Holcombe replaced John, he continued the support. The Bank of Travelers Rest and the president, Bruce White, always made gifts each year to North Greenville. Mr. White made sure their support remained strong, then and now.

And although I am sure I have not mentioned some important supporters, I would be remiss if Vernon Powell was not recognized for his consistency and perseverance in giving to North Greenville. He did not have much financially that he could give, but he gave sacrificially and on a more regular basis than most over the years. Jim and John Ramsey of Diamond Hill Plywood Company, George Bomar, and Jim and Patt Fero were givers. These people, and many others, have continued to help the university improve, which goes a long way in being a good influence as a giver.

Through the years I have to admit that God has looked very favorably on North Greenville University. At the same time, we tried to seek His face in all things.

When you look at growth, ability to succeed through extreme difficulty, and now as a school that people seek out, North Greenville has developed a reputation for quality education, integrity, and being true to the gospel. Thank God for the influence of others through giving on the life of North Greenville, and on my life.

Jesus said, **"I know you can't, but I can!!!"**

Chapter 9
WHAT GOD CONTINUES TO DO!

When I look at North Greenville, first of all, I have to admit, when I was there the first time as vice president of different areas, I didn't know that I would do it a second time as president. I certainly didn't realize that God could work through me for the wonderful successes we had over the years. At this time (2013), I think it is appropriate to mention what God has done. NGU exceeded the 42.7-million-dollar Capital Campaign. Originally, we started a 25 million, G.I.F.T God Campaign (Give it Forward to God Campaign), and in five years we were going to celebrate the school being here 125 years. In 2 ½ years, the Lord blessed and we reached our 25-million-dollar goal. The Board of Trustees said we have 2½ more years left on the campaign, so let's have a Hallelujah Goal of $42.7 million dollars. The $42.7 million was exactly what we needed to move the university forward. There was no fluff in the goal. In the campaign we were talking about scholarships, endowment funds, many facilities, and programs that were all needed. NGU surpassed that goal and the campaign would eventually be completed in 2015.

We have got to remember that the most impressive thing about the facilities at North Greenville is how much they didn't cost. Also, we have to remember that North Greenville built and renovated over $60 million in buildings over the past 20 years and did not borrow any funds to pay for them. **When you cannot explain it, you know it's of God**. In addition, because we had our own construction team and many individuals and companies donated their time, materials, and supplies, the costs were significantly less than expected. In the summer of 2013, Carpenters for Christ from Alabama (over 175 men and boys) came to the campus and helped build two 72-bed residence halls. This saved over $300,000 per residence hall.

Because of the fundraising success and unique construction process, we were able to transform the campus through new, fantastic facilities without any debt. Since 1991, the Lord has performed many miracles in our fundraising, which has made a tremendous difference in our success. The following development history adequately records His handiwork:

Development History

Academic Year	Total Gift Amount
2013-2014	$ 9,811,575.42
2012-2013	$ 7,890,369.05
2011-2012	$ 6,700,357.12
2010-2011	$ 3,417,205.29
2009-2010	$ 3,129,929.91
2008-2009	$ 4,893,225.05
2007-2008	$5,334,801.44
2006-2007	$ 5,239,618.93
2005-2006	$ 5,110,470.05
2004-2005	$ 5,237,578.43
2003-2004	$ 4,280,803.55
2002-2003	$ 4,353,741.54
2001-2002	$ 3,040,890.00
2000-2001	$ 2,514,085.36
1999-2000	$ 4,001,067.59
1998-1999	$ 3,040.918.68
1997-1998	$ 3,539,862.52
1996-1997	$ 2,099,443.57

1995-1996	$ 2,561,686.59
1994-1995	$ 1,431,831.03
1993-1994	$ 1,522,093.35
1992-1993	$ 1,195,070.37
1991-1992	$ 517,602.62
1990-1991	$ 308,716.51

In 2013, our plans were to begin in the near future the following: a new science building, an arena/worship center, an equestrian center, a country store with a Papa John's Pizza in downtown Tigerville, a football turf field, a renovated baseball stadium, 12 tennis courts and complex, a softball turf field, an all-purpose turf field, a track, an athletic weight-lifting building, and a drive-thru coffee shack, in addition to the two residence halls already mentioned. So you see, many, many opportunities were developed because of our fundraising efforts. The only thing that continued to cause us problems was the time it took to get permits to build. It seemed like it was getting more and more difficult to acquire the necessary permits.

I am reminded of a humorous version of the story of when the Lord spoke to Noah. The conversation between the Lord and Noah went something like this:

> *"In the next six months, I'm going to make it rain until the whole earth is covered with water and all the evil people will be destroyed. But I want to save a few good people, and every kind of living thing on the planet. I'm ordering you to build Me an Ark."*
>
> *And in a flash of lightning, he delivered the specifications of the ark. "OK," said Noah, trembling in fear, and fumbling with the blueprints.*
>
> *"Six months, and it starts to rain," thundered the Lord. "You'd better have my Ark completed, or learn to swim for a very long time."*

And six months passed. The skies began to cloud up and rain started to fall. The Lord saw that Noah was sitting in his yard, weeping. And there was no Ark.

"Noah," shouted the Lord, "where is my Ark?"

A lightning bolt crashed to the ground next to Noah. "Lord, please forgive me!" Begged Noah. "I did my best, but there were big problems.

First, I had to get a building permit for the Ark construction project, and your plans did not meet code. So, I had to hire an engineer to redraw the plans.

Then I had a big fight over whether or not the Ark needed a fire sprinkler system.

My neighbors objected, claiming I was violating zoning by building the Ark in my front yard, so I had to get a variance from the city planning commission.

Then I had a big problem getting enough wood for the Ark because the "SAVE the SPOTTED OWL" group has a ban on cutting trees. I had to convince the US Fish and Wildlife that I needed wood to save the owls. But they wouldn't let me catch any owls. So, no owls.

Then the carpenters formed a union and went out on strike. I had to negotiate a settlement with the National Labor Relations Board before anyone could pick up a saw or a hammer. Now we have 16 carpenters going on the Ark but still no owls.

Then I started gathering up animals, and got sued by the animal rights groups. They objected to me taking two of each kind.

Just when I got the suit dismissed, the EPA notified me that I couldn't complete the Ark without an environmental impact statement on your proposed flood. They did not take kindly to the idea that they had no jurisdiction over the conduct of a Supreme Being.

Then the Army Corps of Engineers wanted a map of the proposed flood plain. I sent them a globe.

Right now, I'm still trying to resolve a complaint from the Equal Opportunity Commission over how many Croatians I'm supposed to hire.

The IRS has seized all my assets, claiming I'm trying to avoid paying taxes by leaving the country.

I just got a notice from the state about owing some kind of use tax.

I don't really think I can finish your Ark for at least another five years," Noah wailed.

The sky began to clear. The sun began to shine. A rainbow arched across the sky.

Noah looked up and smiled.

"You mean you're not going to destroy the earth?" Noah asked, hopefully.

"No," said the Lord sadly, "Government already has."

Although this story is quite humorous, unfortunately it has been very real as we tried to obtain the necessary permits to build facilities.

We were always looking at new programs and were excited about our plans for a Physician's Assistant Program. We wanted to provide Physician Assistants because we believe that is the way for the future, more so than Medical Doctors. It was a three-year accrediting process.

We were also looking at strong online undergraduate and graduate programs. We believed we could reach two, three, four thousand more students over the next five years, especially non-traditional students, with the online program. It would be easier to grow the institution in that direction, instead of having to add more residence halls and more buildings on the campus. But we also believed that when we promote the online program, it will increase and enhance our traditional program, our residential and commuter programs on our main campus, and our graduate programs.

Another planned program addition was an Animal Science academic major with an equestrian emphasis. We had begun the work on the necessary facilities that would board horses as well as the necessary classrooms. The program would lead to an equestrian competition team that would compete on the national level.

We were looking at many other programs, and were always trying to see what God sees while trying to seek His guidance in adding new facilities and new programs. As we looked to the future, we wanted to continue trying to stay focused on the Lord. We were averaging over 300 students and campers each year accepting Jesus Christ on the campus. Over the last 24 years, we had over 6,000 people accept Jesus Christ, and only God knows how many more accepted Jesus Christ off our campus through all our different programs. We continued to do more for Him on and off our campus and be changers of the world.

> A wealthy man and his son loved to collect rare works of art. They had everything in their collection from Picasso to Raphael. They would often sit together and admire the great works of art.
>
> When the Vietnam conflict broke out, the son went to war. He was very courageous and died in battle while rescuing another soldier. The father was notified and grieved deeply for his only son.
>
> About a month later, just before Christmas, there was a knock at the door. A young man stood at the door with a large package in his hands.
>
> He said, "Sir, you don't know me, but I'm the soldier for whom your son gave his life. He saved many lives that day, and he was carrying me to safety when a bullet struck him in the heart and he died instantly. He often talked about you, and your love for art." The young man held out this package. "I know this isn't much. I'm not really a great

artist, but I think your son would have wanted you to have this."

The father opened the package. It was a portrait of his son, painted by the young man. He stared in awe the way the soldier had captured the personality of his son in the painting. The father was so drawn to the eyes that his own eyes welled up with tears. He thanked the young man and offered to pay him for the picture. "Oh, no sir, I could not repay what your son did for me. It's a gift."

The father hung the portrait over his mantle. Every time visitors came to his home, he took them to see the portrait of his son before he showed them any of the other great works he had collected.

The man died a few months later. There was a great auction of his paintings. Many influential people gathered, excited over seeing the great paintings and having an opportunity to purchase one for their collection. On the platform sat the painting of the son. The auctioneer pounded his gavel. "We will start the bidding with this picture of the son. Who will bid for this picture?"

There was silence.

Then a voice in the back of the room shouted, "We want to see the famous paintings. Skip this one."

But the auctioneer persisted. "Will somebody bid for this painting? Who will start the bidding? $100, $200?"

Another voice angrily shouted, "We didn't come to see this painting. We came to see the Van Gogh's, the Rembrandts. Get on with the real bids!"

But still the auctioneer continued. "The son! The son! Who'll take the son?"

Finally, a voice came from the very back of the room. It was the longtime gardener of the man and his son. "I'll *give $10 for the painting." Being a poor man, it was all he could afford.*

"We have $10, who will bid $20?"

"Give it to him for $10. Let's see the masters."

"$10, this is the bid, won't someone bid $20?"

The crowd was becoming angry. They didn't want the picture of the son.

They wanted the worthier investments for their collections.

*The auctioneer pounded the gavel. "Going once, twice, **SOLD** for $10!"*

A man sitting on the second row shouted, "Now let's get on with the collection!"

The auctioneer laid down his gavel. "I'm sorry, the auction is over."

"What about the paintings?"

"I'm sorry. When I was called to conduct this auction, I was told of a secret stipulation in the will. I was not allowed to reveal that stipulation until this time. Only the painting of the son would be auctioned. Whoever bought that painting would inherit the entire estate, including the paintings. The man who took the son gets everything!"

God gave his son 2000 years ago to die on the cross. Much like the auctioneer, His message today is: the son, the son, who'll take the son?

Because, whoever takes the Son, gets everything.

"For God so loved the world that He gave His only begotten Son, that whoever believes in Him, should not perish but have everlasting life." John 3:16. That's love.

Now that's what is wanted in the future at North Greenville. I want to see the school continue to share the gospel and always want one more saved. It needs to continue to send more students out onto the mission field than all the other schools combined, and to reach the world for Him. That's the future - more important than programs and buildings. If just one more gets saved, the school can close down today, because that makes it all worthwhile. But I will always want it to be about one more; so therefore, I want it to keep moving forward for Him with **hugs (love).**

I am reminded of one of my most favorite stories of all. The mother was at the creek on the bank sunbathing. As she was lying back in her lounge chair, she was reading her book, taking in the sun, and watching her little boy in the creek, having the greatest time splashing. All of a sudden, she heard the worst scream that every mama in the world would hate to hear. The little boy screamed out, "Mama, Mama, Mama, please help me!" The mama looked up and an alligator had her son by the legs, pulling him out into the deep. Just like every mother would do, regardless of the danger, she threw down her book, jumped in the water, grabbed hold of her little boys' arms and it was a tug of war. Back and forth, back and forth. Don't ever underestimate the perseverance of a mom. Mom won out and saved her little boy, but not without some real lacerations up and down his legs. He had to go to the doctor and have many operations.

After a couple of years of surgeries, he and his mom were visiting a doctor and checking out all the scars and how his legs had gotten better. The doctor said, "You can be proud of all those scars on your legs. They are nothing to be ashamed of. You can be proud of them, and you should be." The little boy looked over at his mom and he looked at the doctor. Then he rolled his sleeves up on both arms. He said, "Doctor, I guess I am somewhat proud of the scars on my legs, but let me tell you about the scars I am most proud of." He put his arms out before the doctor and said, "The scars I am most proud of, are the scars right there on my arms where my mother's fingernails dug into my wrist to save my life."

You see, the scars I am most proud of, are the scars at the wrist area of my Lord and Savior, Jesus Christ, where He hung on that cross to save a sorry, good-for-nothing person like myself. And all I have to do is believe.

During the 2013-2014 academic year, nine mission teams traveled to South America, Central America, South Asia, Central Asia, Middle East, Sub-Saharan Africa, Eastern Europe, and San Francisco, California. There were many others under consideration. North Greenville needs to remain a Great Commission University that's unswervingly committed to the task that Christ gave us to make disciples of every nation. Do not stop until every person has heard about Jesus Christ.

And Jesus said, **"I know you can't, but I can!!!"**

Great Commission Sculpture on Campus

"'Go therefore and make disciples of all the nations, baptizing them in the name of the Father and of the Son and of the Holy Spirit, teaching them to observe all things that I have commanded you; and lo, I am with you always, *even* to the end of the age.'" Amen."

Matthew 28:19-20.

Chapter 10
CELEBRATING LIFE BY SHARING JESUS

I realized when I became president of North Greenville, that many times when you ask God, you need to be prepared for His answer.

Here's a great story about when Grandma goes to court – lawyers should never ask a Mississippi grandma a question if they aren't prepared for the answer. In the trial, a southern small-town prosecuting attorney called his first witness, a grandmotherly, elderly woman to the stand. He approached her and asked, "Mrs. Jones, do you know me?" She responded, "Why, yes, I do know you, Mr. Williams. I've known you since you were a boy, and frankly you've been a big disappointment to me. You lie, you cheat on your wife, and you manipulate people and talk about them behind their backs. You think you're a big shot when you haven't the brains to realize you'll never amount to anything more than a two-bit paper pusher. Yes, I know you."

The lawyer was stunned. Not knowing what else to do, he pointed across the room and asked, "Mrs. Jones, do you know the defense attorney?" She again replied, "Why, yes I do. I've known Mr. Bradley since he was a youngster, too. He's a lazy bigot, and he has a drinking problem. He can't build a normal relationship with anyone, and his law practice is one of the worst in the entire state. Not to mention he cheated on his wife with three different women. One of them was your wife. Yes, I know him. The defense attorney nearly died.

The judge asked both counselors to approach the bench and, in a very quiet voice, said, "If either of you idiots asks her if she knows me, I'll send you both to the electric chair."

Perhaps you should not ask the question if you are not prepared for the answer.

Also, as president, I wanted to be sure the Lord didn't have to look for me when it came to serving and allowing Him to make the difference.

A telemarketer called a home one day and a small voice whispered, "Hello?" "Hello! What's your name?" Still whispering the voice said, "Jimmy." "How old are you Jimmy?" "I'm four." "Good. Is your mother home?" "Yes, but she's busy." "Okay, is your father home?" "He's busy, too." "Well, I see. Who else is there?" "The police." "The police? May I speak with one of them?" "They're busy." "Any other groups there?" "The firemen." "May I speak with a fireman, please?" "They are all busy." "Jimmy, all those people in your house and I can't talk with any of them? What are they doing?" "Looking for me," whispered Jimmy.

It was evident that I, not as the president, but as one called by God to serve, needed to be ready for His answer and His whisper. Therefore, I would like to share the mission trip that my wife and I and a friend took to India. I asked the question, "Should we go?" And although I didn't like the answer, I knew very clearly that God wanted us to go. He didn't have to look for me when it came to serving and being a part of missions.

Dr. Sam Thomas and Dr. M. A. Thomas, his daddy, who has since passed away, have an organization called "Hopegivers International." They have a lot of schools and orphanages and are doing such a good ministry in India. They had asked us to go, and after much prayer we felt like the Lord expected us to go, so we did. Our purpose was to go over and work with the orphanages and schools. I was to speak at the graduation for their different seminaries and ministries. Bottom line - just try to represent the Lord as best as we could. We were not aware that things were tenuous in India, especially northern India.

When we arrived in India, we were met by some of the Hopegivers International people. They had someone there to meet us and make sure we were doing what we were supposed to do, as well as travel safely. We were going to the northern part of India, in an area called Kota. I started noticing that something strange was happening. There were people watching us and there were folks bothering us more than normal. Our supervisor and/or tour guide, the ones that were driving and taking care of us, were a little more anxious about things than I thought they should be. When we finally arrived at Kota where the compound was located, for our work with the different ministries, I heard that some of the graduates traveling to Kota had been beaten up. One or two had been killed. They were being persecuted for their faith and their beliefs. It became obvious to me that there were some real problems and that our lives could be in danger. I didn't want to alarm Gretchen or our friend, so I kept it to myself. I talked to our guide and he was concerned. They didn't feel like there was a real danger for us with two or three of them being with us. They felt like they could somewhat protect us.

When we arrived at the compound and were looking around, trying to get our bearings as to what we should be doing, Sam Thomas came to me and said that my life would be in danger if I got up and spoke at the graduation. They were going to need to tape me speaking. They would show a video of me speaking that night at the graduation instead of me speaking in person, because they didn't want me to risk my life. God didn't send me to India to hide, so I told Sam very boldly and clearly that I felt God would want me to speak as well as be a part of this ministry the whole time I'm here. I would not accept speaking through a video. I would do it in person, even if it meant that I would lose my life. (I am sharing this story, not to bring any special recognition for myself, but I wanted it to be all about our Lord and Savior, Jesus Christ. I am hoping to show how He protected us and how He can overcome adversity through this experience.)

Things never got any better. More folks were injured or harmed on the way there. They were trying to protect as many people as possible. I tried to keep this away from my wife and our friend as much as I could.

On the night of the graduation, they were to have 10,000 people in attendance - many of them were graduates with their families and friends. I would be speaking and sharing Jesus Christ at this graduation. They had tents that looked like they would cover two football fields. There were easily 10,000 or more people who did make it in spite of the danger. It confirmed even more, if these people could get there and risk their lives, the least I could do was risk mine. I didn't have any choice!

The armed guards were out in front of the compound. They were standing there determined to keep me from going in. I turned to my wife and said, "Look, your life could be in danger. We could send you back to where we are staying, but I'm going to speak. They will have to arrest me or kill me, but I am going into the compound and do what I came to do." God expected me to represent Him at this graduation. She said, "No, I am going with you." She made a tough decision in a very quick moment. The car pulled up and we got out. It was as if God just took over and clamped the arms down of those soldiers. It was just as if they didn't notice us. We walked right through them and there was a gate to get into the compound. They opened the gate and we were able to get through. I will never forget being in the compound and I was, to say the least, relieved. I was more concerned about my wife and our friend than I was myself. I was hoping I hadn't put them in a bad situation.

The evening came and they had the homemade lights up and the homemade tents. It was packed. There were people everywhere. The graduation ceremony started and it became my time to speak. When I got to the part of the message involving the scripture passage - John 3:16, "For God so loved the world that He gave His only begotten Son, that whoever believes in Him, should not perish but have everlasting life." The place went completely black. The power had been turned off.

I stood there, and I admit I was very scared. But at the same time, I knew God was in control. I just stood frozen. I didn't budge. I just waited for the next shot, the next pop, the next noise or something like that to happen. It wasn't five minutes, but it seemed like an hour before the lights came back on. When they did, the Hopegivers International people had surrounded me at that very moment when the lights went out and I didn't know it. If anything had happened, they had shielded me from any danger. I thought about that. They risked their lives for me. I wasn't worthy. Tears coming down my face, I continued with the message that God had given me. We ended up having a good graduation.

We had many problems trying to get back to the airport, traveling on the train. God sent angels through people that surrounded us all along the way. He got us back safely to the airport and back home. As I look back on that experience, I realized that many missionaries and many people risk their lives every day. I am ashamed that I have not done more for my Lord. I also remember standing there when the lights were out, remembering a verse – Philippians 1:21, "For to me, to live is Christ, and to die is gain." It was time to become a difference maker. It was time to stand up for Jesus.

After returning, I never told that story publicly to anyone. As a matter of fact, I didn't say much about it because I wanted it to be between God and me. I didn't want to take any credit. Then, Sam Thomas came for graduation at North Greenville and he told the story. It was really the first time that story had been shared. Although I did nothing and God did it all, I really wanted it to be more about Him. Sam brought and presented to me what is called, "The Martyr's Pledge," which I was not worthy to receive. It went like this:

"Being of sound mind and body, I do solemnly declare this martyr's pledge without any persuasion or enticement." It said some other things, but I will never forget how it started. "I solemnly declare this martyr's pledge." I thought, am I really a martyr? There was no comparison between me and all the other missionary folks who gave their lives so people could hear about Jesus Christ. What an honor! What an honor to go out and share Him with others even if it means risking your life.

Although I have had a near death experience trying to serve Him, it's still very difficult to accept death. Even when you know that the person is going to be in Heaven. You want to celebrate that life. The most difficult thing of all is to have to go and tell parents or students or friends that a loved one has died or a friend has died. Through the years at North Greenville, we had a number of students whose lives ended on this earth. I wish I could share more about all the students, but will only share the complete stories of a few.

Back in the 80s when I was vice president, there was a sweet young lady named Sandy Blackmon. She had gone home at the end of the semester and someone took her life. It was my first experience with a student's death and it broke my heart.

There was Nancy Dunston, who was in a car with another student coming back to campus and was thrown from the car and killed. This death occurred a year or so after Sandy's death, and was just as difficult to handle.

Then, Rick Barnes was coming back to school late one night from studying off campus and hit a tree in a car accident and didn't make it. I was devastated because he was an outstanding young man and student.

There was James Russian, who knew he had health problems, but he wanted to be at North Greenville and go to school as long as he could. He died right there on campus. Although we knew of his health complications, we did not expect his untimely death and would have encouraged him to be with his family. But he felt better about being with his North Greenville family. His death really hurt me.

Then, we had three students riding in a car, going to serve the Lord. The road that runs in front of the campus is called Highway 414. You take Highway 414 three miles from the campus and you will arrive at Highway 25. Highway 25 will take you toward Asheville, North Carolina, or to Greenville, South Carolina. But, when you get to Highway 25, at that time there was just a stop sign at the intersection. There was a lot of traffic and it was difficult to cross. I had sent letters many times, asking the DOT to put a red light there. It was difficult for not only students, but community people to get across. They just wouldn't do it. And it took the death of two more students.

They pulled out in front of an 18-wheeler that hit the car. Shawn Boyd and Rachel Cooler, who were boyfriend and girlfriend, went on to be with the Lord. They were headed with Pierre Salmon, another student, to a church to minister and serve the Lord. Pierre lived and wasn't hurt too badly. He made the best of it. He has gone into ministry and serves the Lord in many ways.

I couldn't help but remember him being in that wreck. God keeping him from being harmed and the other two being killed. It really came to mind when at a later date he was singing a beautiful song at my son's wedding. I started to see a little more clearly why Pierre's life was saved. He has allowed God to make a difference through his life. But, on that particular night of the accident, I must admit asking God, "Why?" There was no real purpose being served by their deaths. I had many questions and few answers.

Then, there was Tiffany Huff. She had a beautiful voice. She was in the Fine Arts program and I loved to hear her sing. She was at that same intersection, but she made it across. She had seen her father that morning to get something from him. On the way back across Highway 25 her car got hit by another car and she went on to be with the Lord. Also, there was Brandon Daniel. He was in a wreck, as well. He was coming back toward the campus when it happened. Again, it hurt my heart to share with their parents, even when I knew these students loved the Lord and were with Him.

Jordan Robinson loved to play basketball and was part of our basketball program. His father was a local pastor. He had health problems, as did Zack Bishop, an art major. Both of these young men tried to go to school with these problems and be involved, but before they could finish, the Lord took them home. At the time, I questioned God about two young men with special gifts being taken so soon. They had so much talent and a lot of love to give. Although I knew all these students belonged to God before they were born, it did not make it any easier to accept.

Then, there was Ryan O'Connell. I will never forget the morning I found out he had wrecked his motorcycle and died. His brother also attended North Greenville. I went over that morning to his brother's apartment and there were a lot of friends and North Greenville people there. I asked his brother, "Was Ryan a Christian?" This is why I am so thankful that we require them to go to chapel. His brother said, "Oh, yes, you know we had to sit beside each other because of our names. I remember the day when the one speaking in chapel asked if you accepted Jesus Christ to raise your hand. That day Ryan raised his hand to accept Jesus Christ." It thrilled my heart to hear this great news, but I still had a difficult time accepting his death.

Brittany Fogg – I will never forget that sweet person. It was Valentine's night and I was going through the residence halls. We usually have a student activity for a couple of hours where the guys come into the girl's residence halls on Valentine's night. I came by her room, hugged her, asked her where her boyfriend was and if he was coming over. She said, "No, he had to work." She was going to go the next day to see him. I hugged her and said, "You know I love you, but God loves you more. We laughed and I went on. The next day, she got on Tigerville Road and Highway 11. I guess she didn't see the vehicle coming and pulled out in front of it. Immediately she went on to be with the Lord. I saw her parents that night at the hospital about 11 pm. Her mom said when Brittany was born, she and her husband gave her to God. She belonged to Him and evidently, God needed her more than the parents did. I was really impressed how they handled it, but the hurt at that very moment was overwhelming.

At the funeral, her Youth Pastor said she gave Christian CDs to the family and all the radio stations in her car were on Christian stations. She had on at her death her "True Love Waits" jewelry. And the pastor said, "You know she wouldn't want to come back. She loves Heaven."

The Pastor used "WWBD – What would Brittany do?" He said first of all, Brittany would tell her Mom and Dad how much she loves them. Then, she would tell all parents how precious their love truly is. Next, she would tell her boyfriend just how special he was to her and don't lose your focus. Then, she would tell all the girls, purity feeds the soul. She said what she meant and she meant what she said. She would then tell graduating seniors to choose college wisely and tell all Christians that serving Jesus Christ is the only way, and the greatest. Her next statement was that God is who He says He is - Genesis 1:1 - There is God. Next, she would tell people God is the answer and that Heaven is real. The last thing she would say is to tell us today is the day to acknowledge sin, turn to Jesus, trusting God by faith."

On her computer, they pulled up all kind of scripture verses and other special items about how she loved Jesus. At the funeral, 30 people were saved and half of them were her family. I began to realize God's purpose through death, and how He can turn any bad situation to His good.

Then, there was Joseph Bunn. I remember the day Joseph and his father came to my office in the middle of summer. I wasn't sure that Joseph was going to come to North Greenville. It was in July, 2003, when he and his father, Alan, came to see me. He decided he wanted to go to North Greenville and we would work it out. I knew Joseph had not been living for the Lord. His mom and dad had been praying for him and were special friends of mine. I will never forget the night I was sound asleep and got the phone call. The Campus Minister mentioned that Joseph Bunn had just been killed in a car accident. He had been thrown from the car and was found underneath when they got his ID and realized it was Joseph. I told him to come by and get me. I would be the one that needed to go and tell his parents. They lived in Greenville, just 30 minutes away from the university.

At this particular time the best route from Greer to North Greenville was undergoing repairs. You couldn't come the more direct, safer route from Greer to Tigerville. Other roads were crooked and curvy. We told the students coming from Greer to take Highway 290, which is a straight road to Highway 25, another good road to Highway 414, which was a direct route to North Greenville. It was out of the way and longer, but it was safer.

Joseph, for whatever reason, decided to take a curvier road that night back to campus and lost control of his car.

The Campus Minister picked me up and we went to Greenville. I knew where Alan lived, so we went to the home and knocked on the door. I remember knocking two or three times and finally, the light came on in the hall. Alan looked out the window with the porch light on, and recognized me. He said, "Jimmy what are you doing here tonight?" I said, "Go get Mrs. Bunn. We need to talk a minute."

He did and they came into the living room where I told them that Joseph had gone on to be with the Lord. Oh, it was so devastating. I'm not sure if Alan said it or if I just heard God saying it, but one way or the other, it became very clear, "God Sure Is Good" came to my mind. How in the world, in a situation like this, could this be said? How could that be the thought? We got in the car, went down to the hospital, and walked down into the lower level with the Bunns and identified the body. They said, "Yes, that's Joseph."

Whether Alan said it or someone said it or I just felt it, I heard, "God Sure Is Good" again. We returned to the house and church people were there. It was buzzing and a time when I thought I was going to help them, I was being touched. I was the one being helped. Again, I heard it, "God Sure Is Good."

It wasn't long until they had their funeral service at church and we had our own Celebration of Life service. Alan and his family were there. They had pictures on the screen, and then Joseph spoke through the media technology. He told about growing up in a Christian home his entire life and was actually baptized at 12 or 13, which made no difference in his life. He went on to say, "During high school, I had been involved in my youth group, but I had come to the point in my life where I was so tired of pretending to be a Christian. My brother would get up early and go to school for prayer group. These kids in the youth group were talking about what God was doing in their lives. I didn't understand it and I didn't really want to be around it at all. I was tired of having to pretend to be a Christian."

The youth group was planning to go to camp for a week in the summer and Joseph's dad encouraged him to go. His dad said, "He felt he should at least talk to God about camp and see if he could still do something in his life. Ask God to show Himself to him." Joseph said, "I just thought that if I ask God to show me Himself, I was going to get in a horrible car accident and that's how God would show me Himself." (To say the least, I was blown away when I heard him mention a car accident.)

Joseph decided to go to camp because he had already paid. Although he reluctantly went to camp, he figured that he could play the games and avoid chapel. But he was forced to be at chapel and the preacher shared about the cross. Joseph said, "I had always heard that the cross was this horrible thing, but to hear it described in so much detail about the pain and suffering Jesus Christ went through for my sins, it was just amazing. It kept bothering me every night." On Thursday night at chapel, Joseph nailed everything to the cross, repented of his sins, and gave his entire life to God. Joseph said, "God broke me and it was a freeing thing. It's so awesome."

Family and friends had been praying that God would change his life. Then he said, "After camp, it was so awesome. What now? I want to grow in God. I've just been praying for God to show me what he wants me to do. He has really put it on my heart to be in Youth Ministry. I just praise God for all the awesome things he is doing in my life. It has been pretty incredible."

On October 26, 2003, roughly two months later, God took Joseph home to be with Him. It was mentioned so clearly at the Celebration of Life service for Joseph, that he had done more for the Lord in those two months since he got saved than most people would have done in years. He was sharing and being involved in the youth group. He was doing all those things to try to get others to accept Jesus Christ and to be a good representative of the Lord. All of a sudden, it became so clear why, "God Is So Good." As in Joseph's testimony where he says, "If I asked God to show me Himself, I was going to get in a horrible car accident."

"God Is So Good." Joseph had time to accept Him. Don't ever underestimate the power of prayer and the love of a Mom and Dad. Yes, "God Is So Good."

Brent Elrod was the last student to go on to be with the Lord during my tenure as president. In October 2013, Brent went hiking by himself near North Greenville in the foothills of the Blue Ridge Mountains. He decided to climb the waterfalls and fell to his death. He had it worked out with his girlfriend that if he went out by himself, she would always know where he could be found. If he didn't call at certain times, she would go looking for him. He didn't call, so she went looking for him and found him face down in the water. She couldn't bring him back to life. He was already celebrating in Heaven. Brent was studying to be a minister and had just preached the Sunday before. Someone had gotten saved and he was fired up for Jesus. He was a student coordinator, part of our Resident Assistant program. It was on a Thursday night in October, 2013. I will never forget going to the home and being with the Mom and Dad. It was devastating to say the least. There were a lot of tears. Our children are supposed to bury the parents, not the other way around.

In this situation, and in all of them, you keep saying, "Why, Lord?" What do you say to the parents? How do you understand the purpose? It's not right to question our Lord, but at the same time, how can you not ask the question, why?

God knew when it was going to happen. He knows everything. He's omnipresent, omnipotent, and omniscient. He's the Alpha and the Omega, the Beginning and the End. Two months before this happened, I went up to see a pastor in Flat Rock, North Carolina, about being on our Board of Trustees. He mentioned that he had a speaker by the name of Tony Nolan coming to do a revival in October at his church. Tony Nolan is a well-known speaker and communicator. College kids love to hear him speak. God can really use him to touch hearts and to get folks saved.

He gave me Tony's number and we scheduled him to speak. I realized that we were on Fall Break and we only had Wednesday of that week because students would be gone on Monday and Tuesday. We have chapel services every Monday and Wednesday at 10 am. Nobody would be here on Monday, but maybe we could work it out for that Wednesday, and God did work it out. I called our Vice President for Campus Ministries and told him we were going to let Tony speak as long as the Spirit moves. Chapel runs from 10:00 – 11:00, but I knew this was going to be a special day and we weren't going to worry about classes. I prayed diligently about it and the Lord was going to use Tony and Brent's Celebration of Life. Brent died on Thursday and students went home on Friday, the next day.

The 10 o'clock chapel on Wednesday was the first time the North Greenville family could be together since Brent's death. Brent's Mom and Dad and family members were there and we sat them on the front row. We were all still very sad about it, but we were also trying to celebrate Brent's life. Tony Nolan was also a spiritual hero of Brent. He would have been tickled to know that the day we celebrated his life, Tony Nolan, his spiritual hero, would be speaking in chapel.

We celebrated the life of Brent, and Tony did a tremendous job of bringing it together. It wasn't an emotional time as much as it was a touching-the-heart time. Around 11:30, Tony had everyone to stand and gave the plan of salvation and told anyone who accepted Jesus Christ to raise their hand. There must have been 100 to 150 that raised their hands. Then he said, "If you are for real, you will come on down front." Probably over 100 came down front. Some of them could have been our own ministry folks, but many of them came down to get saved. God knew two months before and He worked it out. He allowed me to be a part of His plan to have the Celebration of Brent's life and Tony Nolan on that Wednesday, so at least one more would get saved. In this case, many, many more got saved.

After the service, I went to see Brent's Mom and Dad, tears flowing down their faces, and they said, "Oh, we better understand." Brent would have been so pleased by all the hearts that were touched that day. Because of Brent's going on to Heaven, and cel-ebrating his life, God sent me a wonderful speaker to go along with it. It was a heart thing completely - a wonderful service and a family coming together. Brent's death certainly was not in vain. The death of all these students, definitely not in vain. Thank the Lord!

So many times, we think about death and life. In death, if we know they are saved, then there is a celebration. But all along the way in life, we've got to know it's about putting God and others first, and putting yourself last, being willing to give of yourself and allow Jesus to make a difference through you.

I read of a little girl who was suffering from a very rare, serious disease. Her only chance of recovery appeared to be a blood transfusion from her 5-year-old brother, who had miraculously survived the same disease and had developed the antibodies needed to combat the illness. The doctor explained the situation to the little brother and asked the little boy if he would be willing to give his blood to his sister. He hesitated only a moment before taking a deep breath and saying, "Yes, I'll do it, if it will save her." As the transfusion progressed, he lay in the bed next to his sister and smiled as we all did, seeing the color return to her cheeks. Then, his face drew pale and his smile faded. He looked at the doctor and asked with a trembling voice, "Will I start to die right away?" Being young, the little boy had misunderstood the doctor. He thought he was going to give his sister all his blood in order to save her, yet he was willing.

Just like the little boy, every parent of these students would say, "Lord, take me instead of my son or daughter." But God already has the plan for every life. God's forgiveness in Christ is complete. The real devastation at death is the question of salvation, and the real celebration at death is knowing that your loved one is in Heaven. For those of us left behind, the results and consequences of sin remain upon our lives.

A certain little boy would lie to his parents. They would give him spankings, they sent him to his room, they would do everything they could to get him to quit lying. Finally, his father went outside and started putting nails in the barn door for every lie the little boy told. After there were dozens of nails in the barn door, it started attracting attention from many people. His father would explain that every time his boy lied, he would put a nail in the barn door. The little boy became very concerned and ashamed

116

so he said, "Daddy, how can I get those nails out of the barn door so people won't know I'm a liar?"

His father said, "Stop lying." If you do it for a month, we will take the nails out of the barn door. On the 31st morning, the little boy couldn't wait. He and his father went out to the barn and his father took all the nails out of the door. When the last nail had been extracted, the little boy stepped back to see the results and then he burst into tears. The father asked why and the little boy said, "The nails are gone, but the marks are still there."

As Christians we continue to fail each other, but Jesus Christ never fails us. Regardless of the marks from the nails in our lives, God sent His son and He loved us so much that He forgives us, if we will only come to Him and repent of our sins. He never, never gets tired of being there for us.

A young man was on the diving team at the university and he was proud of the fact that he was an atheist. He would always challenge the Christian people about their faith and would always make fun of them. They stood toe to toe in arguments about it. He loved to go to the pool and dive. One night, he went to the swimming pool at the university. He went up on the diving board and he was getting ready to dive. It was dark in there, but there was just enough light coming from the moon through the windows. He couldn't see down but he could sort of see the wall behind him and up higher. He got to the end and turned on the end of the diving board with the toes on both feet on the edge of the board to do a back flip off the board.

When he raised his arms and got everything just perfect with his toes on the end of the board, the moon was shining in such a way that it put a shadow that looked just like Jesus hanging on the cross. He had debated his Christian friends so many times and they had told him so many times about Jesus being on the cross and hanging there for his sins. When he saw that shadow of his body with his arms out and it looked like Jesus on the cross, he went down on his knees and he begged for forgiveness and he realized that he needed to give his all to Jesus Christ. When he stood back up to dive once he got things right with God, he turned to dive into the pool, a maintenance worker walked in and cut the lights on and hollered, "Please, please, please don't dive," just in time. When the young diver looked down, the pool had been drained and there was no water.

I have talked about the surviving, the stabilizing, and the thriving of North Greenville University, and how North Greenville was converted into a Christ-centered school, committed to allowing Jesus Christ to make a difference as well as being passionate about it. Also, I've tried to make it clear that it's not about me, but it's about Him. Perhaps, it shows the sense of humor of our Lord and Savior, Jesus Christ, when He had me as president of North Greenville University. Those who do know me, know that I don't have the capability, and God put me in that position so it would be even more clear that He had to do it…that I couldn't.

North Greenville University is not mine. It doesn't belong to the faculty, staff, students, or even the board of trustees. It belongs to our Lord. As long as the school stays focused and seeks His face, then and only then, will one more continue to get saved on the campus, and one more continue to get stronger in their walk, and one more continue to graduate. Combine all three into one and you have a very unique university that is quite different from most schools.

As Jesus continues to say, **"I know you can't, but I can!!!"**

Chapter 11
GOD WORKS IN EVERYTHING FOR OUR GOOD

The year 2014 was the greatest year in the history of North Greenville University and was the last year of my presidency. We had thoroughly enjoyed serving 36 years at the school (12 as a Dean and Vice President and 24 as the President). At the November 6, 2014, Executive Committee of the Board meeting, we celebrated the success through Jesus Christ in spite of me and others.

We started the meeting with the Development and Advancement area reporting through the GIFT (Give it Forward to) God Campaign Steering Committee, that we had surpassed our $42.7 million goal (this included gifts received, commitments, and deferred gifts.) This wonderful result did not include a $60 million anonymous estate planning gift. Only a couple of development employees knew about it, because I did not want the donors to be slack in their giving with such a huge commitment. We had decided to announce the total amount raised (over $107.4 million) in 2015 at the GIFT God Campaign Celebration. The following is the March 31, 2015, report with two months left in the campaign:

Gift God Campaign Report
June 1, 2010 - May 31, 2015

	Gifts Received	Commitments	Deferred Gifts	Total	Goal	% Achieved
Addition to Endowment for Scholarships					$8,000,000.00	152.29%
CMSF & Missions	$1,630,060.60	$16,790.00	$631,530.00	$2,278,380.60	$2,000,000.00	113.92%
Academics	$157,112.00		$500,000.00	$657,112.00	$2,000,000.00	32.85%
NGU Financial Need Based Grants	$4,713,261.59		$4,500,000.00	$9,213,261.59	$2,000,000.00	460.66%
Athletics	$34,600.00			$34,600.00	$2,000,000.00	1.73%
Epting Athletic / Worship Center					$10,250,000.00	103.03%
Lobby with Concession Area	$134,500.00	$231,333.00	$1,150,000.00	$1,515,833.00		14.78%
Arena	$93,100.00	$200,400.00		$293,500.00		2.86%
President's Box	$211,711.35	$38,288.65	$250,000.00	$500,000.00		4.88%
Men's & Women's Dressing Rooms	$93,100.00	$90,440.00	$100,000.00	$283,540.00		2.76%
Other	$4,958,591.21	$1,283,740.00	$1,725,000.00	$7,967,331.21		77.73%
Academic Village at Tigerville					$4,250,000.00	17.59%
Academic Offices & Classrooms	$682,470.50	$50,000.00		$732,470.50		17.24%
Local Business Opportunities						
Dining & Shopping						
Increased Profile for Village	$15,000.00			$15,000.00		0.35%
Science Building Renovation / Addition					$2,500,000.00	131.58%
Lecture / Computer / Animal Rooms						
Laboratories / Research Areas	$171,805.00			$171,805.00		6.87%
Offices / Storage Rooms / Break Rooms						
Other	$1,231,318.25	$9,100.00	$1,877,539.00	$3,117,957.25		124.71%
Residence Halls	$1,052,925.84			$1,052,925.84	$2,500,000.00	42.11%
Athletic Complex Additions					$1,000,000.00	147.84%
Softball Complex, locker rooms & offices	$70,000.00	$50,000.00		$120,000.00		12.00%
Practice fields for soccer and track	$280,488.18			$280,488.18		28.04%
Tennis complex w/offices & locker room	$286,034.92			$286,034.92		28.62%
Undesignated Athletic Complex	$776,765.26	$15,000.00		$791,765.26		79.18%
Building Endowment	$0.00			$0.00	$750,000.00	0.00%
Operations						
Undesignated Campaign Funds		$182,375.00	$2,070,000.00	$2,252,375.00		
Other						
Misc. Operations	$6,083,719.04		$250,000.00	$6,333,719.04		
Non-endowed student scholarships	$4,644,934.01			$4,644,934.01		
Misc. Endowment	$22,983.27			$22,983.27		
Misc. Plant	$3,974,495.51	$517,500.00	$315,922.50	$4,807,918.01		
TOTAL	$31,318,976.53	$2,684,966.65	$13,369,991.50	$47,373,934.68	$42,700,000.00	110.83%
						3/31/2015

Although this was fantastic news, nothing compared to the excitement of people getting saved! From June 1, 2014, through November 6, 2014, 252 people had received Jesus Christ on campus, a number that does not include many who were saved through ministry and mission teams off campus. We cannot forget that Jesus said, **"I KNOW YOU CAN'T, BUT I CAN!!!"** It was always so much fun watching Him show out through our people and programs. Also, in September 2014, we held our best Global Mission Week ever, with 732 students, faculty, and staff responding to the call. Out of the 732, there were 13 professions of faith, 246 commitments to short term mission projects, and 473 committed to longer mission projects.

As the meeting progressed, it was reported that the Fall 2014 semester saw the largest undergraduate and graduate enrollment in university history. There were 2,372 undergraduate students and 265 graduate students for a record total of 2,637 students.

The Executive Committee reviewed the current budget of $53,934,097, as well as the proposed budget of $56,793,933, which included tuition, room, and board costs for a full-time student for 2015-2016 at $25,930. This cost was the third lowest among private schools in the state, which meant the university provided quality education at a bargain cost. The proposed budget included a 3% salary increase and covered all the employees' benefits, something God had enabled us to do for over 20 years.

The new programs for the 2014-2015 academic year were the Equestrian and Animal Science Programs, the Physician Assistant Program, the College of Adult and Professional Studies, and a new Physical Education degree (a K-12 Teacher Certification Degree). Also, we maintained a student-to-faculty ratio at 15 to 1, and added 16 new full-time faculty members for the Fall 2014 semester.

The committee was definitely pleased with the November 4, 2014, bank balance of $19,068,564.60, which would exceed $20,000,000 in February 2015. This was the exact amount of the university's cash on hand in the different local banks.

Our auditors had reported recently that "North Greenville University was in rare air compared to others financially." They made it clear that the university's strength was the finances, and the school was in the top 1% of the schools and ministries they audit. Very few, if any of them, were so soundly managed as North Greenville.

In Development and Advancement, it was reported that the fund-raising year ending May 31, 2014, saw the highest gift amount in the history of the school. The total was $9,811,575.42! The endowment had grown to $26,137,822, and the Christian Ministry Scholarship Fund as of November 6, 2014, had 436 members and an endowment of $3,580,752.91.

It was reported that two 72-bed residence halls had been completed along with a football turf field, an all-purpose turf field, 12 tennis courts and complex, and an athletic weight-lifting facility. Property had been acquired for the Equestrian/Animal Science Programs, an all-purpose building had been erected on it with a fence surrounding it, and a number of horses had been donated to the program. North Greenville personnel were working on the Tigerville Country Store, which would be the anchor store for our planned main street with several other stores and businesses. A grading permit had been obtained and bids were being accepted for the track and softball turf fields. Gifts and/or commitments had been received to begin the new science building, the Arena/Worship center, and to renovate the baseball stadium with a turf field. There were also many more prospective donors to see about helping fund these new facilities. Meanwhile, plans were underway to upgrade and renovate many current facilities, especially residence halls. Many renovation projects had already been completed, but the renovation of current facilities never stopped.

SINCE 1991, OVER $60 MILLION HAD BEEN SPENT ON OUR NEW AND RENOVATED FACILITIES AND NORTH GREENVILLE UNIVERSITY HAD NO DEBT! THANK YOU, JESUS!

No one will ever be able to take away the great joy and fulfillment I had while serving our Lord over 36 years at North Greenville. I am a humbly blessed example of the saying, **"Although God can do it by Himself, He delights in allowing just anyone to be a part of His success."** I never imagined that in my life He would call and allow me to make a difference through my service. The main thing was being available and willing.

The best decision of my life was accepting Jesus Christ as my Lord and Savior and walking down the aisle at an early age in Green Hill Baptist Church, West Columbia, South Carolina, to let the pastor, my dad, know of my decision. I made it clear that I believed Jesus Christ died on the cross for my sins. I asked forgiveness, repented of all my sins, and turned to Him. I knew that three days after Christ died on the cross He rose from the grave and lives, so I can live forever in Heaven with Him. There was no question that I was born again. I grew up being a South Carolina Baptist preacher's kid and was proud of it.

During my early years in West Columbia, my best friend was a dog named Blackie. We played together every day and he stayed in the back yard surrounded by a fence. I will never forget the Christmas when Santa brought me a brand-new cowboy outfit. I was so excited, and after getting dressed from head to toe with the outfit, I went outside into the back yard. Blackie did not recognize me so he attacked. He basically ripped the outfit off me until he heard my screams. Then, standing over me, he began to lick my face. Regardless of the loss of a special Christmas present, how can one get upset when you know that your best friend loves you unconditionally? It is amazing the many life lessons one can learn from a dog.

Since my dad was called to build South Carolina Baptist churches, we moved a few times and I attended high school in Rock Hill, S.C. I will always remember when Blackie killed the annoying dog next door. He had gotten old and his tolerance level was low. My parents felt it necessary to end his life. Finally, after a lot of heated discussion, they compromised and drove him an hour from home to release him. I still vividly recall the tears flowing down my face and with a broken heart seeing Blackie standing on the side of the road as we drove away. Another lesson is life is not always fair.

My father as a pastor truly suffered for the Lord. We were poor. But even that taught me valuable life lessons. At the age of 13, I began working at the Rock Hill YMCA, and the Executive Director of the YMCA, Robert Hope, became one of my second dads. During high school, I also delivered *The State* newspaper and was responsible for delivering to the whole town, which was smaller than it is now. I would start work at 4 am because it took at least two hours to deliver the papers. Since the local police knew I had to finish in time for school, that I was the local preacher's kid, and played sports, they mercifully never stopped me for running all the red lights and stop signs. Trust me, at four in the morning I was the only one on the roads.

I was making more money than my parents, which was necessary in order to pay for my sister's college education. Also, I knew I needed to do well with my grades and become a good athlete in order to obtain scholarships for college. There was no question that my parents could not afford to cover any college costs. Therefore, my day started at 4 am with the paper route, followed by school until 3 pm, ball practice from 3 pm to 6 pm, and working at the YMCA until 9 or 10 pm. In 2 Thessalonians 3:10 it says, "For even when we were with you, we commanded you this: If anyone will not work, neither shall he eat." I learned at an early age the importance of one's willingness to work and work hard.

When I graduated from high school, I was fortunate and received athletic and academic scholarships to attend college. Also, after finishing high school, I never lived with my parents again. They moved to another church in another city and I wanted to continue my work at the YMCA. Mr. Hope went out on a limb for me and allowed me to live in the health spa area in the YMCA during college breaks and the summer. To say the least, there were many times when being the only one in that huge facility was quite scary, and my relationship with the Lord became stronger. Mr. Hope was demanding and sometimes expected more than was realistic. But he had a good heart and cared for and loved others. Throughout my life I have tried to be a lot like Robert Hope.

After college, I married the beautiful girl I met during my junior year in college, Gretchen Moore. (We have been married since 1973 and I love her more today than I did then.) I received a fellowship to pay for my master's degree and doctorate, and my sweet wife worked to help pay the bills. We continue to be soulmates and partners and, whatever I have accomplished, I owe to the Lord and my wife.

I remember one day when she and I took our car to the shop to get the brakes fixed. The mechanic came from under the car with grease all over his clothes and told us where to park the car. He mentioned that, since he was good friends with Gretchen, he would get to work on it immediately. When we got home, I asked her about this friendship and she informed me that she had almost married him. I chuckled and said, "Well, if you had married him, you would be the wife of a greasy mechanic." She smiled and said, "If I had married him, he would have been the president of the university." Another lesson learned! It makes a tremendous difference when the one who you love not only supports, but works with you in making the difference for Jesus Christ through your service for Him.

North Greenville University reached a new level of excellence in 2014, and we give God the credit and praise for it all. But, God used a South Carolina Baptist preacher's son, known as a country boy and a redneck, who made himself available. When you add to God's guidance the experience and lessons from life, miracles can happen.

In the Bible, the book of Job tells the story of a man of God. Job was a prosperous farmer who owned property and thousands of livestock in the land of Uz. His faith could be matched by no one. God allowed Satan to test Job and his faith. It was devastating how Satan assaulted Job and his life built on God. But never underestimate the sovereignty of God. After Job lost all his possessions, his health, and his children, as well as suffered the betrayal of his friends who claimed he had sinned, he maintained his innocence and trusted God through it all. And God was enough.

In no way, shape, or form do I compare myself with Job. But I sometimes reflect and think that I have had just a glimpse of what Job experienced. I have no idea why things happen the way they do, but God does. He remains sovereign. As my life began to unravel and I began to feel persecuted from all sides, I did my very best to trust and lean on God regardless of what happened.

In late 2013 and early 2014, I began working closely with three vice presidents concerning the development of a new undergraduate online program and the strengthening of our graduate online program. We traveled a lot together as we reviewed the programs at other schools. Also, the administration spent a lot of time together with strategic planning for the programs. We felt that the future of the school depended on a strong online program to accompany all the current programs. There was significantly more communication and interaction in 2014 between my staff and me concerning this opportunity than in the past.

In late June and early July 2014, tension and conflict brewing within my own family erupted and crossed over into my work at North Greenville University. I reluctantly share this only because it is an integral part of this story. Omitting it would leave this telling incomplete in ways that could suggest or imply incorrect interpretations and conclusions about these events. It was at this time that my daughter and her husband falsely accused me of having a sexual affair.

They did their very best to convince my sons and my wife. It seemed incredible that they could come to this conclusion from their home in Texas. We did not typically see them more than about three weeks out of the year.

When they first got married, they lived in Florida and had many problems. Then, we helped get her husband a job in Greenville, S.C., living near us, and their marriage seemed to get better. After a few years, her husband took a job in Texas. They demonstrated what we saw as a serious lack of respect for each other. The strain in their relationship was enormous. When her husband took the job in Texas, our daughter was determined not to go with him. She said she was ready to end the marriage.

Finally, Gretchen and I strongly encouraged her to join her husband in Texas, with the understanding that we would agree to allow her to come back to Greenville after one or two years, with or without him, if they could not make it work. I have sadly felt it necessary to practice tough love with them in dealing with problems and concerns in their marriage over the years. Although I do not pretend that I always handled things perfectly, my sincere desire out of love for them and their children was to see them grow together in a marriage pleasing to God, and through which their lives would reflect Jesus and draw others to Him. Instead, they developed serious resentment toward me and harbored a lot of bitterness and anger. By November 2014, it reached the point where they would not talk to me and our daughter verbally abused her mother constantly. To say the least, it had become an unhealthy situation between all of us.

In their efforts to prove that I was having an affair, they trespassed (unlawful entry) into our home and stole my iPad, hacked into my cell phone for texts and e-mails, had a trail camera set up at my other house, (our primary home was a university-owned and provided house), and worked it out to have a GPS locator placed on my vehicle. They tried to convince my sons of the alleged transgressions, and my sons became willing to participate because they wanted to find the truth. Their motivation was different from that of their sister and her husband. They were not willing to accept assumptions, innuendos, and opinions as truth.

On October 30, 2014, I had planned to spend a couple hours at my house to work on my boat. The employee in question needed to discuss the upcoming Online Program Board Meeting in California with me before she and her husband left the next day to travel to that meeting. Since ours was not a planned meeting that day, I asked her and she verified that her husband knew about it. We worked the entire 30-minute trip to the house. Once there, I worked on the boat dock while she sat on the porch and worked. When I finished, we stepped into the house so she could use the bathroom and I could get something to drink.

That is when I heard someone come up the stairs from the basement and became concerned that an intruder had broken into the house. When I went to confront the intruder, it turned out to be my son, Paul, who, as part of his effort to figure out the truth of his sister's accusations, was video recording what he found. It clearly surprised me when I saw Paul, and when he barged into the bathroom, it terrified the employee. We had not been in the house for more than five minutes and, as the video showed, we were fully dressed and were not acting inappropriately. The video shows my innocence of the accusations rather than any guilt.

My son, Paul, who took the video, said the following in an affidavit he submitted to the NGU board: "From day one of our concern about my fathers' transgressions, I have only sought out the truth, whatever that may have been. My brother Bert and I, in agreement with our sister and brother-in-law, did make the decision to track our father with a GPS device. We also placed a trail camera at his house to take video/pictures of anyone coming and going, which I could check every week. As for the video, I was seeking the truth. Why else could I have made the video? It was meant to uncover the truth, NOT cover it. This is where my brother and I adamantly disagree with my sister and brother-in-law. The video speaks for itself. My father and the employee were scared, but fully dressed about to head home. My father even went as far as to give us a signed letter that his neighbor watched him earlier that day, working at the dock on the boats. There was no proof or evidence of any sexual interaction of any kind, just them at the house together. My sister and brother-in-law would like for you to believe that my father and the employee had a sexual encounter while at the house, but again that is pure speculation supported by a lack of evidence. These are the facts of that situation."

On November 8, 2014, we had a family meeting with my daughter and her husband via facetime. In this meeting my daughter and her husband accused me of bribing the family and accused Paul, Bert, and Gretchen of "covering up my sins." My daughter and her husband had no basis for attacking the character and integrity of the entire family by insinuating they were manipulated, and too weak to ultimately make up their own minds and hold me accountable.

My son, Bert, said the following in an affidavit he later submitted to the NGU board: "We have worked tirelessly to find something of substance to not just accuse our father, but show his transgressions. We participated willfully in tracking, videoing, and photographing all my father was doing in an attempt to find the truth. What we found was nothing more than my father working too much, a father who had let work interfere with his marriage and family, a father who was blinded to the hurt of his family, but also a father who genuinely cares, supports, and loves his family with all he has." At the end of the facetime family meeting, everyone agreed to revisit the matter in January, 2015, but on November 9, 2014, my daughter and her husband began calling board members in order to share their false accusations, misconceptions, assumptions, and innuendos, as well as show them the video.

At this point, I prayed to Jesus and again told Him that I cannot do this, and He said, **"I KNOW YOU CAN'T, BUT I CAN!!!"** The Bible verse, Romans 8:28, came to mind. It says, "And we know that all things work together for good to those who love God, to those who are the called according to His purpose." It reminded and reassured me that **GOD WORKS IN EVERYTHING FOR OUR GOOD**. God allowed all of this and He is going to use it. I said to Him, "I trust You. I may not like it, but You know best." God is working to fulfill His purpose and not necessarily to make us happy. It became clear to me that God is able to turn every circumstance (good or bad) around for our short and long range good.

Over the next several weeks our daughter and her husband worked closely with some board members, and the family was informed that they would be coming to a special meeting of the board on December 30, 2014. Our two sons and their wives tried at least twice to talk them out of coming to this meeting. Finally, they told them, "We have tolerated all you have done currently against our father, but we will not accept your attendance at this meeting!" "If you come to this meeting, both of you will no longer be a part of our family, so please do not come!"

Gretchen and I were invited to the December 30th meeting and when we arrived, we could hear our daughter and her husband testifying against me from outside the room where the meeting was taking place. **IT BROKE OUR HEARTS!**

From the beginning of the ordeal to the end, I was never advised by the board of any actual charges against me. However, **I was cleared of any sexual misconduct and did not violate any school (employee) policies.**

When the December 30th meeting was adjourned, three board members were assigned to meet with Gretchen and me. They informed us that no decision concerning my future had been made and we agreed to meet in our home after the first of the year, 2015, for further discussion.

However, by this time our hurt was enormous and we no longer wanted to be at North Greenville University. Also, we did not want to keep fighting and cause division among the board. We loved North Greenville and had given our lives serving there. We desired to protect the school and its reputation from conflict and controversy, so the university and its ministry could continue moving forward. Additionally, we needed to try and salvage what was left of our family. We realized that, if we kept fighting, the hurtful truth about the problems between our daughter and her husband and the struggles within our family would eventually surface and destroy any chance we still had to repair and restore relationships. Ultimately, North Greenville was God's university and we did not want His ministry to get hurt. Many people would like to see a Christ-centered school fail to measure up to His standards. We decided to take a sabbatical for the spring semester and then retire. We certainly appreciated the diligent efforts of the three board members who met with us in early 2015 in making this happen.

On January 5, 2015, I saw the employee and told her, "Your job is safe and I will be retiring tomorrow." (More than four years later, she continues to be employed by North Greenville University.) She looked me in the eyes and said, "I told you I would do whatever I had to do to save my boys and my job." Right then and there, I realized that one day I would need to clarify all that had happened. **(MY FAMILY AND I, IN A CHRISTIAN SPIRIT, WOULD WELCOME THE OPPORTUNITY TO DISCUSS THE FACTS AND EVENTS WITH THE EMPLOYEE AND HER HUSBAND AND TRY TO MEND OUR FRIEND-SHIP. ALSO, THE EMPLOYEE AND I NEED TO ASK EACH OTHER'S SPOUSE FOR FORGIVENESS!)** Since that day, I have not engaged in any contact with her except one time about three weeks later when I accidentally saw her and her son on the way to an athletic event.

On January 6, 2015, Gretchen and I met with the full Board of Trustees. I apologized and told them I regretted my poor judgement and would immediately resign as president of North Greenville University. We agreed I would take a sabbatical from January 6, 2015, through May 31, 2015, and that I would officially retire on June 1, 2015. **THE 25 MEMBERS OF THE BOARD GAVE US A STANDING OVATION AS WE LEFT THE ROOM.**

What soon emerged was a complaint against me for sexual harassment with this same employee. It was confusing, disappointing, and hurtful to Gretchen and me because she and her husband had willingly supported and been a part of my defense at meetings with board members and administrators in November and December, 2014. There was further confusion and hurt because she had been a good friend with my wife and me for over 20 years.

Just a few months earlier, she had called Gretchen wanting to meet with her. Gretchen had her over to our home and she shared with Gretchen about her strong friendship with me. Gretchen forgave her and befriended her. Gretchen's Christ-like action touched my heart. Because this employee had always been a fine person who was good at her job, I could not help but wonder if she had been pushed or coerced to do this, or if her job had been threatened in a way that led her or those advising her to conclude that this was the only way she could protect that job.

The sexual harassment complaint, though, was a serious matter. At this time, during former President Obama's administration, sexual harassment complaints were enforced in ways that carelessly and dangerously deprived the accused of basic rights – no right to counsel, no opportunity to examine the accuser or other witnesses, not even a whiff of what most would consider fundamental fairness. Due process was handled loosely and many were convicted merely on an accusation.

In spite of the unfair restrictions imposed by the Obama Administration on those who are accused under this law, North Greenville University did a tremendous job of discovering the truth and handling the sexual harassment accusation fairly and correctly. On March 5, 2015, I was told that it had been determined the interactions between the employee and me were **NOT** sexual harassment. It was satisfying and a relief to finally be cleared of sexual misconduct accusations and to be able to move on with my life.

After I was cleared of any sexual harassment accusations in March, 2015, I started hearing that she and her attorney were trying to convince people that she had done no wrong and I was to blame for everything. It would serve no constructive purpose to disclose all the details of what was said or done during this time. The real underlying issues, though, concerned our friendship in the workplace. I had certainly come to the point where I recognized and admitted that I had to accept responsibility and blame for my poor judgement.

There was no affair, no harassment, and no school policy violations. However, we had allowed our working relationship to develop into a strong friendship that created a perception of preferential treatment. It would be farcical for anyone to believe that this was one-sided, or that this employee was not at least an equal partner in the friendship. And after working together for more than 20 years, any other person working with us would have to admit that we had each contributed to any perception of preferential treatment between us. But I ultimately recognized that, as I had done, this employee would need to sort out for herself what responsibility and blame might belong to her; that would be between her and God, and did not need to further concern me.

During this time, I was spending more and more time in God's Word. Studying Genesis 36 through 50 about the story of Joseph spoke volumes to me about my experience. Joseph experienced many hardships. He had relationship problems within his family for which he took some of the blame. Joseph was falsely accused of sexual misconduct. He endured a long imprisonment and others forgot or did not appreciate what he had done for them. But he continued to stay positive, remained faithful to God, and moved forward. He did not waste time asking God why all of this was happening to him. At every setback he knew God was with him. After spending significant time studying about Joseph, I realized that in all things God is indeed with me, shedding light on even my darkest days. Just as He did with Joseph, I can trust that He still has a plan and purpose for me.

On February 20, 2015, I received a call from Bert's wife, Hannah, informing me that Bert and two of my grandchildren had been run over by a car. Then she said she did not know whether they were dead or alive. Immediately, Gretchen and I left for their home in Rome, Georgia. About an hour down the road, Hannah called back with the news that Bert had a concussion and a cracked sternum. She also said that my grandson, James, had a concussion and should wind up okay, but my granddaughter, Campbell, was on her way to have brain surgery in Atlanta. We were stunned.

We learned that Bert and the children had walked down the street from their house to check out a wreck when another car that had not been involved in the original accident came up and jumped the curb. It knocked Bert more than 30 feet from the point of impact and then ran over James and Campbell. Little Campbell survived the surgery and has a metal plate in her head, but did not suffer any brain damage. And, thank the Lord; all three of them have recovered well.

Being retired gave us time to help them through this crisis. Having that time to help them was a blessing in disguise and a very good reminder to us that God is always good. If He allows it, He is going to use it. We are not always going to understand what happens in life or why it happens. We still need to trust God. All of Joseph's bad breaks were part of God's plan. My family and I embraced this time as part of God's plan for our lives.

On Wednesday, April 29, 2015, the University hosted our retirement celebration. It started with the President's Quartet singing and my preaching in Chapel. I was thrilled to see the chapel full of students, faculty, and staff, especially since the students did not receive chapel credit for this special service. The most exciting and satisfying part of the day was seeing five students accept Jesus Christ. But, if it had been just one, it would have been worth it all. We had a great reception afterward and everyone made us feel very special. Some of my special friends, independent of the board or the university, gave me a new Toyota Avalon! Wayne Landrith, the vice president for Development and Advancement, was responsible for a great day and had raised funds for the new car. During his employment at North Greenville, he had done a great job of assisting me in fundraising. The entire day was special and it gave us a wonderful feeling of closure to our time at North Greenville University. Now, Gretchen and I could move forward in seeking God's plan for the next phase of our lives.

Meanwhile, I had begun in January of 2015 to work with search firms that indicated I was very marketable as a candidate for president of another school, especially one that might be struggling. But that ended in August when, seemingly overnight, my reputation became severely tarnished. On August 27, 2015, a video surfaced anonymously on YouTube. It raised questions and implied allegations about the circumstances that led to my retirement. The video went viral. As soon as I learned about it, I called the university's lawyer at that time about sending out a joint release in order to share what really happened. But they would not do it.

I learned that the South Carolina Baptist Convention leaders suddenly and understandably had a lot of questions about the matter. However, no one from the convention leadership tried to contact me about it. This proved disappointing to me, as one would have thought they would want to know all sides of such a story before coming to any conclusions. I had given the majority of my life to South Carolina Baptists and, as a result of God's blessing on my work, South Carolina Baptists had a vital and viable Christian university they could be excited about rather than a failed and closed school. I had been with hundreds of Baptist ministers in their churches over the 36 years at North Greenville. However, after the video came out, I heard from no more than 20 of them. Even thinking the worst of me, one might think a Christian brother might have called and said, "I am praying for you and, if you need anything, do not hesitate to contact me."

I came to understand in whole new ways how important it is for a pastor or any Christian to take time to be compassionate toward others, regardless of the circumstances, and to always try to love others through the challenges in life. If you add some mercy and grace to that love, which is what Jesus Christ has done for us, you can make a tremendous difference in that person's life and bring glory to our Lord. I also came to realize that I had become derelict of my Christian responsibilities toward others during my time at North Greenville. I had plenty of excuses for not checking on someone who was hurting. After all, I was very busy and had a lot of responsibility. But I am so grateful that God has never used any of those excuses on me.

The news media quickly jumped all over the story about the video and showed how little they cared about the truth. They took advantage of the word "allege," which enabled them to spread fake news or shady news as a smear tactic. When you say allege, you are making an assertion without proof. When the media reports say allege, they are making assertions without proof. The media coverage was farcical, to say the least. I was surprised and appalled by the innuendos, rumors, and rush to judgement that accompanied the media stories surrounding the allegations.

All too often, people are wrongly convicted in the court of public opinion on the basis of false, misleading, and incomplete information, long before all the facts are presented so the truth of the matter can be known. The media reporting quickly became noise rather than news. I also realized that the media was actually less interested in me, personally, and more interested in using the allegations to undermine the reputation of North Greenville University and the work of Christ through His school. I came to see the larger spiritual battles and warfare that were going on behind the twist and turns of my own story.

As a Christian leader, I certainly exercised poor judgement at times, made mistakes, and did things wrong. I am continuing to learn from my shortcomings. I am also hopeful that I may be able to help others avoid similar mistakes, yet show them Christ's love, mercy, and grace when they fall short and go through challenging times of their own.

There are valuable and wise lessons to be drawn from my last year as president of North Greenville University, both for the Christian leader and also for anyone who desires to serve God effectively.

First, I became obsessed with the passion of focusing on serving Jesus Christ at North Greenville. I had drifted away from being obsessed with the passion of focusing on serving Jesus Christ **ONLY**. There was a difference. In my mind, Jesus Christ and North Greenville grew to become one and could not be separated. Nothing else mattered and that was not healthy. I was going to get the job done whether it meant being with one employee or 100 employees. It was success at all costs. The bottom line was, in the end, it became more about me than about Him; more about **MY** passion than about Him being the object of my passion. As a result, my family suffered, I exercised poor judgement and made costly mistakes, some people were hurt and others became disillusioned; and Satan had a field day stirring up rumors, innuendo, lies, resentments, pride, anger, conflict, and divisiveness among God's people. I had started to think "I can;" but the truth is, as Jesus said, **"I know you can't, but I can!!!"**

Second, I obviously spent too much time alone with a female employee. I exercised poor judgement that allowed room for critical and suspicious perceptions. We should always strive to set a good example and never give someone reason to think the worst from our actions. I fell short. Before doing anything, we should always ask ourselves, "What is the best that could happen?" But we must also ask, "What is the worst that could happen?"

Third, my leadership style involved loving others. I would touch through hugging and saying words of encouragement like love, appreciate, and care. I never hesitated to hug anyone, male or female, friend, acquaintance, or employee. To some, I am told, this was almost like my signature or trademark, something I was known for by almost everyone who was around me for any amount of time. One friend has recently shared with me that he might have felt offended and assumed I was upset with him if I had ever seen him without giving him a hug or telling him I loved him.

However, I should have been more careful about telling people "I love you." And I should have been more sensitive to the possibility that someone might misunderstand or misconstrue my hugs and what I intended as uplifting comments. This is especially true in this modern era where false assumptions, innuendo, and untruths travel faster than ever before, where values without foundation are constantly shifting, where people have become addicted to scandal, and where the media and others, even some who claim to be brothers and sisters in Christ, seek and devour that which they would destroy.

Fourth, I always thought I could fix it. I am reminded of the minister who asked one of the older farmers in attendance at the men's breakfast one morning to say the prayer. The farmer began, "Lord, I hate buttermilk." The pastor opened one eye and wondered to himself where this was going. Then the farmer said, "Lord, I hate lard." Now the pastor was worried. But the farmer prayed on. "And Lord, you know how much I don't care for raw flour." As the pastor was about to stop everything, the farmer continued, "but Lord, when you mix 'em all together and bakes 'em up, I do love those fresh biscuits. So, Lord, when things come up we don't like, when life gets hard, when we just don't understand what you are saying to us, we need to just relax and wait until You are done fixing, and probably it will be something even better than biscuits. In Jesus name, Amen."

Whether we are young or old in our ministry or walk with Jesus, we need to let God fix it. He will not mess it up. In Isaiah 43:2 it says, "When you pass through the waters, I will be with you; and through the rivers, they shall not overflow you. When you walk through the fire, you shall not be burned, nor shall the flame scorch you." If we let the Lord go with us, we will grow stronger and He will protect us. If we go in our own strength, we will stumble, fall, and not make it; we will harm ourselves and will harm others along the way.

Fifth, we must constantly examine our own hearts while extending mercy and grace to others. In Matthew 7:1-5 of God's Holy Word, Jesus tells us to examine our own motives and conduct instead of judging others. In verse 5, He says, "Hypocrite! First get rid of the log from your own eye; then perhaps you will see well enough to deal with the speck in your friend's eye." John 8:1-11 makes it clear that Jesus stands ready to forgive any sin in our lives. Verses 7 and 8 state, "So when they continued asking Him, He raised Himself up and said to them, 'He who is without sin among you, let him throw a stone at her first.' And again He stooped down and wrote on the ground.'" Perhaps, Jesus wrote the words "grace" and "mercy." If I have learned anything from this experience, it is that I should throw down my stones and do some serious self-examination before judging others. And when I do judge others, I should seek to give the mercy and grace I so strongly desire from the Christ who has delivered that for me.

In 2014-2015, I felt in some small ways like Job. I believed I was trying to do the right thing, but the worst was happening. But God has a plan! Everything good and bad in life unfolds according to His sovereign plan. I realize even more today, as I continue to experience this in new and varied ways, that I can trust God because He is faithful. God will never leave or forsake me. Even in the darkest hours, He never has and He never will. Jeremiah 29:11 says, "For I know the plans I have for you, declared the Lord, plans to prosper you and not to harm you, plans to give you hope and a future." I have claimed that promise in the past, I am claiming that declaration in the present, and I will claim His word until I meet Him face to face when He calls me to be with Him.

I cannot complete this chapter, **"God Works In Everything For Our Good,"** without saying that God has been so good to give me a wife and life partner in Gretchen who is patient, kind, longsuffering, and whose life displays the fruit of the spirit. We look forward to what God has planned for our future lives and ministry, to a future with faith in God who gives us hope. God is not finished with us yet. I am also thankful for the close, loving, and satisfying relationships we enjoy with our sons and their families. We continue to pray for healing in the broken relationship with our daughter and her husband. We will never stop loving her and we know that nothing is impossible with God. **"I know you can't,"** says Jesus, **"but I can!!!"** I want to set the record straight by affirming my belief that God invented **"HUGS"** so we can let people know we love them without saying anything. And, last but not least, I pray for God's rich and continued blessing on North Greenville University, where Christ makes the difference.